Severn Bridge Junction and Abbey Foregate: A Class 66 passes with a Portbury Dock to Rugeley power station MGR coal train.
ALL PHOTOGRAPHS TAKEN BY THE AUTHOR UNLESS OTHERWISE CREDITED.

Introduction

A seismic change is sweeping across Britain's Railways. As large if not larger than the abolition of steam is the implementation of the Network Operating Strategy or NOS.

This blueprint for the next 10 years has two strands. On the one side is the policy of concentrating the signalling of the UK in 12 railway operating centres (ROCs). The second pillar of the strategy is the European Railway Traffic Management System (ERTMS) which allows cab signalling and problem solving in the face of delays or accidents.

The concept of a 'bunker' controlling thousands of miles of railway is not new. More than 15 years ago, staff from Railtrack (the predecessor of Network Rail) visited the US and were impressed by the control bunkers used by the Union Pacific and BNSF railroads. These two massive western railroads have a single signalling and control centre for their entire 20,000 mile-plus networks.

The UP's bunker is in Omaha, Nebraska, and the BNSF has a similar facility in Fort Worth, Texas. Inspired by what they saw, Railtrack staff returned and plans were drawn up for the first UK ROC at Saltley. The building was completed but there was no money for resignalling, so the concept was shelved. A decade later, Saltley is busy taking over the signalling of the West Midlands and will eventually itself be merged into the Rugby ROC currently under construction.

Putting a lever back in the frame 'under careful supervision' – the author at work. The observant may see the cover of the author's 1986 book, British Rail in Camera, above lever 15.

The driving force behind the ROC strategy is, of course, the savings on salaries. In the industry this is known as 'opex' savings, or operational expenditure savings. Is it worth it? To try and answer this question it is helpful to consider a couple of examples. When the Norwich to Ely line was resignalled in 2012 the staff count was reduced from 52 to six. Similarly the resignalling of the lines from Norwich to Yarmouth and Lowestoft will see a reduction in staff from 70 to just six signallers. Looking at the national picture, these savings would suggest that the

CONTENTS

Author:
Michael Rhodes

Designers:
Fran Lovely, Tim Pipes

Reprographics:
Paul Fincham

Production editor:
Dan Sharp

Publisher:
Tim Hartley

Publishing director:
Dan Savage

Commercial director:
Nigel Hole

Printed by:
William Gibbons and Sons, Wolverhampton

ISBN: 978-1-909128-64-4

Published by:
Mortons Media Group Ltd,
Media Centre,
Morton Way,
Horncastle,
Lincolnshire
LN9 6JR
Tel: 01507 529529

ABOVE: *Attleborough*: The fascination with signalling and signal boxes spreads well beyond the enthusiast community, perhaps a reflection of the heritage stored up in so many Victorian buildings? Here, in 2012, shortly before closure, my mother and father get a demonstration of how a signal box works, given by David Hilton in Attleborough signal box.

RIGHT: *Denton Junction*: This March 1984 view of Denton Junction signal box was originally pleasing because of the gas lamps that were still in action. This 1888 LNWR box had a 54 lever frame at the time, but later in 1984 this was reduced to 18 levers. Levers Nos. 37 to 54 were kept and renumbered 1-18. As this publication was being developed this picture took on renewed significance as the signaller on duty back in 1984 was Anthony MacIntyre, who is now the LOM for the Peak Forest area. Fast forward from 1984 to 2013 and a chance meeting in the Peak District revealed that Anthony remembered me and had lost his copy of this photograph. How much easier it was to scan and email the image than it had been to package up an 8x10 black and white print back in 1984.

LIST OF ABBREVIATIONS

ABP	Associated British Ports
ARS	Automatic Route Setting
ATP	Automatic Train Protection
AWS	Automatic Warning System
CCTV	Closed Circuit Television
DMI	Driver Machine Interface
EMU	Electrical Multiple Unit
ENIF	ERTMS National Integration Facility
EOR	European Operating Rules
ERTMS	European Railway Traffic Management System
ETCS	European Train Control System
GNER	Great North Eastern Railway
GPR	General Purpose Relief
GSM-R	Global System for Mobile Communications – Railways
IECC	Integrated Electronic Control Centre
IFS	Individual Function Switch Panel
L&SWR	London & South Western Railway
LIDAR	Low level radar
MGR	Merry Go Round coal train
NTC	National Train Control
NX	Entrance Exit Panel
OCS	One Control Switch Panel
PSB	Power Signal Box
RETB	Radio Electronic Token Block
ROC	Railway Operating Centre (sometimes Regional Operating Centre)
SC	Signalling Centre
TMS	Traffic Management System
TOC	Train Operating Company
TPWS	Train Protection & Warning System
UNISIG	Union of European Signalling Companies
VDU	Visual Display Unit

reduction in signallers is likely to be from 5000 to 500. Thus 4500 jobs where the average salary is £30,000 per annum suggest a potential saving of £135 million per annum.

There is also an additional factor which is often overlooked. In 1948, when the railways were nationalised, British Railways had a programme to replace as many pre-Grouping signals as possible with a standard BR semaphore. Fast forward 60 years and many of these posts and signals are in need of replacement. Because the nationalisation programme spawned a drive for standardisation, the concentration of renewals in the 1950s is now coming home to roost.

A second driver for change is ERTMS (European Railway Traffic Management System) which potentially saves large amounts of money by resolving service disruptions and providing a platform for cab signalling and the abolition of all trackside signals.

ERTMS has two components. The European Train Control System (ETCS), or cab signalling, allows the removal of trackside indicators with the signals in the locomotive cab controlled from the new ROCs. Alongside the cab signalling is a new traffic management system (TMS).

This is especially helpful if delays occur. The old method for resolving delays and disruption relied on the local knowledge of signallers or regional controllers.

The new TMS runs hundreds of computer algorithms to decide how best to return traffic to normal timings. To do this the computer takes account of the crew diagrams, locomotive and coaching stock deployment and any restrictions in infrastructure such as line speed.

By electronically looking at all the train paths, the programme allows predictions of exactly when all services will be back on time and thus gives accurate information about when any given disruption will be resolved for the first time.

Not only does the system accurately predict recovery from disruption, but it can also allow inputs from signallers and controllers who may choose to enter their own suggestions to speed traffic up. The computer predicts within seconds if such action will improve or worsen the eventual return to normality.

It is the Traffic Management System that looks certain to bring the biggest savings. As train operating companies levy heavy penalties for delays, Network Rail can potentially reduce these fines substantially using TMS.

ACKNOWLEDGEMENTS

In a project as wide-ranging as this there are many people to thank. Railway staff all over the country have welcomed me to their signal boxes and allowed me to record them at work – the biggest thanks goes to all of them for tolerating my visits. In particular I am indebted to Trevor Maxted, Anthony MacIntyre, Alex Fisher, James Skoyles, James Wells, John Stocks, Tim Randell, Mark Jamieson, Andrew Frost, John Illingworth, Adrian Quine and, most crucially, Steven Ashling.

This publication had its origins some years ago when Steven was the operations manager for West Anglia and asked if I would help him produce a celebration of the manual signalling between Ely and Norwich (www.blurb.co.uk/books/2574300-norwich-to-ely-the-end-of-an-era). The project was well received and has led to other work with Network Rail and ultimately to this overview covering the whole of Britain.

Writing about signalling is a dangerous business when there are so many experts on the subject. To that end I have found the work of the Signalling Record Society invaluable and the help of its members has been crucial, in particular that of David Allen. Background reading and reference material is listed below.

Palumbo, Maurizio. **The ERTMS/ETCS signalling system** published by www.railwaysignalling.eu, 9A Devonshire Square, London ECM2 4AE. 2014.
Kay, Peter. **Signalling Atlas and Signal Box Directory (Third Edition)** published by Signalling Record Society, Wallasey, 2010.
Bridge, Mike. **Track Atlas of Mainland Britain (2nd edition)**, published by Platform 5, Sheffield, 2012.
Kitchenside, Geoffrey, Williams, Alan. **Two Centuries of Railway Signalling**, published by OPC, Sparkford, 1998.
Minnis, John. **Railway Signal Boxes – A Review**, published by English Heritage, Fort Cumberland, Portsmouth, 2012.

Because of these potential savings the recent changes to the Strategic Plan have seen power signal boxes moving into the ROCs earlier than some of the smaller manual boxes.

The traffic management system is being trialled in Upminster power box at the moment and it is hoped to be up and running in the new ROC at Cardiff by 2019 and also the King's Cross panel box. Cab signalling is already in use along the Cambrian Coast line with control based at Machyllech. The European ETCS is being trialled in a Class 313 electrical multiple unit on the Hertford loop and will be introduced on Thameslink next year.

The downside of this rapid change is of course the demise of hundreds of Victorian-era signal boxes. Disappearing with them is a way of life going back over 100 years, that of the signalman (for most were men). From the manual crossing gates to the paraffin lamps in the signals, everything will vanish.

The signal boxes themselves are regarded as important parts of the countryside by English Heritage and fortunately 89 boxes are already listed and consideration is being given to listing a further 68 examples around England. As well as explaining the changes taking place on the railway today, this publication will look at the life and times of over 200 signal boxes all over Britain. Some signal men have been persuaded to add their recollections over 40 years to my own to give a flavour of how life 'used to be'.

Much of the information contained in it is, however, the result of hundreds of signal box visits made over 40 years, starting back in 1974 at Heath Junction in the Cardiff suburbs.

In the last three years, with so many signal boxes due to close soon, I have visited more than 300 and information gathered during this time has been invaluable. As always, any errors in the content are entirely my own.

Thanks must go to my parents who are to blame for the genes that led to a fascination with railways. It was not until a couple of years ago that my mother finally got her wish to see a signal box in action, thanks to David Hilton. This was in Attleborough box.

Finally thank you to my wife who puts up with this railway obsession and who has to be bribed with hot tea and a traditional coal stove to enter a signal box!

Michael Rhodes
Attleborough, March 2015

Sheringham West: My wife Irene watches the goings-on having been lured into Sheringham West signal box by the promise of a warm fire and a nice cup of tea. Erstwhile chairman of the North Norfolk, Steven Ashling, is in residence during the March 2014 gala. The signal box here was formerly Wensum Junction, which closed in March 1987 when an NX panel was installed to control the easterly approaches to Norwich and access to the newly created Crown Point locomotive depot.

The history of signalling

From Hand signals and Time Interval Working to ROCs and ERTMS

SECTION 1
HAND SIGNALS AND TIME INTERVALS TO ABSOLUTE BLOCK AND INTERLOCKED MECHANICAL SIGNAL BOXES.

When the Manchester to Liverpool Railway opened in 1930, the telegraph did not exist and the only way to get a message from one station to the next was on the train itself or perhaps by horseback, racing the train along the line. In these circumstances trains operated on the "time interval" principle. That is to say, if a train arrived at a station, then the signal man would flag the train to stop if the previous train had left just a few minutes before. Once five or ten more minutes had passed the signalman would allow the train to pass on the assumption that the previous train was far enough away to avoid collision. The flaws in this method of working are fairly obvious, but in the absence of the telegraph it was the only way to run the railway in the 1830s and 40s. The hand signals given by the signal man (who often doubled up as local policeman or security officer for the railway), were soon replaced by mechanical devices in the shape of diamonds or spheres. Then in 1841, the first semaphore signal appeared at New Cross on the London to Croydon Railway, and signals we would recognise today quickly became standard on the railway.

In the 1860s, mechanical engineers developed interlocking on the signal frames that controlled points and semaphores to make it impossible for the signalman to set up conflicting routes and there by cause collisions. The first such frame was developed between 1856 and 1860 by a Mr. Saxby and installed at Kentish Town Junction. Shortly thereafter, signal boxes were constructed around the signalling frames. The first of these was at London Bridge and designed by Saxby and Farmer, a name made famous over the next century and a company who's signal boxes can still be found on the network today. So by the mid-1860s the railway had interlocked signal frames, housed in signal boxes, but it was still for the most part operated on the "time interval" principle.

At the time that the Manchester to Liverpool Railway opened there were experiments with a new system called the telegraph. The system used a zinc battery which, when connected caused current to flow along insulated wires and induce movement of a metal needle up to a couple of miles away. In 1837, Cooke and Wheatstone, the inventors, demonstrated the telegraph on the line between Euston and Camden. Here the incline out of Euston had a 1 in 70 gradient and was rope worked. The telegraph was used to alert the rope incline operators at Camden when a train was connected to the system and it was safe to start winding. The system worked but fell into disuse within a year because of failures in the insulation around the wires. Another system installed by the Great Western between Paddington and West Drayton was similarly afflicted and abandoned. Interest in and uptake of the telegraph was patchy to say the least and electrical failures commonplace.

In my only image of permissive block in action, Class 37 No. 37279 creeps up behind a second freight train north of Radyr Yard in March 1977. Unusually, both trains are made up of empty mineral wagons. The guard's van on the right is at the rear of the afternoon trip from Nantgarw washery, which was hauled by Class 08 No. 08349, while 37279 is bringing empties back from Abercwmboi washery.

In spite of the unreliability of the telegraph, the system showed promise, when in 1845 the L&SWR conducted a demonstration game of chess between staff at Nine Elms and Portsmouth, using the device. Still the telegraph was not popular and it was probably not until the announcement of the birth of Queen Victoria's son was made by telegraph that the device captured the public imagination. Furthermore the capture of a murderer using the telegraph to transmit his description from Slough station to Paddington where he was apprehended helped accelerate the use of the device on the railway. In the 1850s, the single Tyer's needle was the system of choice on most railway telegraphs and it became the standard device used for signalling within a decade of it's introduction. The problem was, it was used as an adjunct to the time interval system rather than as the primary train control. Thus the telegraph might be used to inform of schedule changes or late running services, but routine train running was still under the "time interval" principle.

All this changed in 1889 when 78 people were killed at Armagh. A holiday train stalled at the crest of an incline, only to be hit by an express running "right time" behind it. The result was the 1889 Regulation of Railways Act. This legislated that absolute block, controlled by the telegraph must be used on all lines. This meant never more than one train in section whatever the time interval between trains. The Act also made interlocking of all signal boxes compulsory (and it

remains so today). In addition continuous braking was made compulsory for all passenger trains. One quirky exception to the absolute block ruling is permissive block. This may sound like a contradiction, but on many freight only lines, especially approaching busy marshalling yards, slow moving freight trains were allowed to stack up in the block, awaiting access to the yard or sidings. This practice continued well into the 1980s and is well shown in the image of the northern approaches to Radyr yard above. Thus by the 1860s, the signal box with interlocking levers and controlling semaphore signals became the standard system across the rail network. Then after 1889, the introduction of absolute block became compulsory throughout the passenger network.

Signal boxes, first introduced by Saxby & Farmer from 1860 onwards, were mechanically controlled, with rodding to the trackwork and wires and pulleys to the semaphore signals. As the railway grew, so the trackwork and signalling became more complex and the limits of a mechanical system were quickly reached. The largest purely mechanical signal box ever constructed was at the south end of York Station called Locomotive Yard Box and it boasted 295 levers. This box was closed in 1952 when the new York "One Control Switch" (OCS) panel box opened replacing a total of 868 levers in eight separate mechanical boxes. This was the beginning of the electrically controlled panel box, further developed as the NX panel, the most prevalent on today's railway. But before the introduction of OCS and NX panels there were several notable developments to enhance the standard mechanical lever frame by adding electrical, pneumatic or electro-pneumatic control systems.

SECTION 2
ELECTRICAL, ELECTRO-PNEUMATIC AND PNEUMATIC MINIATURE LEVER FRAMES.

For more information on these systems readers may find the following website useful: **www.wbsframe.mste.co.uk/public/index.htm** All three systems for mechanisation aimed to replace the direct wire pull between the signal lever and the semaphore (or indeed the rodding between the lever and the points). In a pure electrical system, the miniature lever in the signal box operated electrical contacts which completed circuits to electrical motors adjacent to the signal or set of points, inducing them to move and change position.

The pneumatic systems in contrast used either mechanical switches or electrical current to switch valves controlling pressurised air, which in turn was used to change points or signals. The first such box by a whisker was at Crewe Gresty Lane, opened in 1899 and purely electrical. Shortly thereafter, the Great Eastern electro-pneumatic box at Granary Junction opened and this was the first to use compressed air to replace manual rodding and wires.

The company that made its name synonymous with the miniature levered power signal boxes which controlled the electrical or pneumatic switches was the Westinghouse Brake & Saxby Signal Company, later shortened to just Westinghouse in 1935.

The company was responsible for the installation of dozens of miniature lever power frames between 1899 and the 1960s, most notably the largest ever frame at Glasgow Central with 374 levers. Opened on Sunday, May 3, 1908, this electro-pneumatic behemoth employed a staff of eight men and four boys, with three signalmen on duty at busy times. The box controlled all track and signals within a 300 yard radius, signalling traffic in and out of the 13 platform Glasgow Central station. The 300 yard radius was important in that it was as far as electro-pneumatic control could reach from this design of signal box.

Beyond this air pressure from the compressor adjacent to the signal box was not sufficient to change points; a severe limitation of the system. The Westinghouse signalling company installed several other miniature lever boxes with over 300 levers as did the General Railway Signalling Company and these are listed in the table below.

There are just three miniature lever frames left in operation on today's railway. At Liverpool Lime Street a Westinghouse L 95 lever frame was introduced in 1948 and was due to keep working until 2015 or 2016. A smaller 47 lever frame survives on the Southern Region at Maidstone East and this too is closing in 2016 when control is to be handed to the Ashford ROC.

The final survivor is Immingham Reception sidings, built by the Great Central Railway in 1912 and operated by the Port of Immingham Authority (ABP). Here a 91 lever electro-pneumatic frame should survive for some years as it is on Port of Immingham land and as yet fails to appear in any of the Network Rail spreadsheets for signal box closures.

It is an unusual box in that in addition to the Great Central miniature lever frame, it contains a 1970 IFS panel to control Humber Road Junction and connections to the coal sidings as well as an NX panel (originally from 1967, but modified in the early 1980s) which controls connections to the Lindsey and Humber oil refineries.

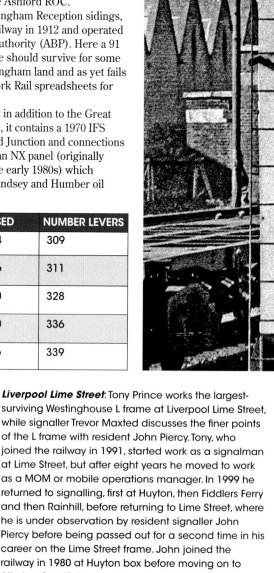

NAME	MAKE	OPENED	CLOSED	NUMBER LEVERS
Waterloo	Westinghouse L	1936	1984	309
London Bridge	Westinghouse L	1928	1976	311
Bristol Temple Meads West	General Railway Signalling	1935	1970	328
Bristol Temple Meads East	General Railway Signalling	1935	1970	336
Cardiff West	Westinghouse L	1933	1966	339

Liverpool Lime Street: Tony Prince works the largest-surviving Westinghouse L frame at Liverpool Lime Street, while signaller Trevor Maxted discusses the finer points of the L frame with resident John Piercy. Tony, who joined the railway in 1991, started work as a signalman at Lime Street, but after eight years he moved to work as a MOM or mobile operations manager. In 1999 he returned to signalling, first at Huyton, then Fiddlers Ferry and then Rainhill, before returning to Lime Street, where he is under observation by resident signaller John Piercy before being passed out for a second time in his career on the Lime Street frame. John joined the railway in 1980 at Huyton box before moving on to Allerton, Sandfields control centre, and then to Lime Street. John comments that in his case the lack of natural light in the Sandfields control centre was the main push for a move to Lime Street. Trevor meanwhile is regaling both men with his time working first at Victoria East and then Waterloo, two of the larger Westinghouse frames built, at 147 and 309 levers, respectively. Lime Street was built in 1948 and has 95 levers in the frame.

Cardiff West: In February 1977, an unidentified Class 47 passes Cardiff West signal box, which was the second largest lever frame ever operated with 339 miniature levers. Only Glasgow Central was bigger.

Maidstone East: The other surviving Westinghouse L frame is at Maidstone East and was built in 1962 with replacement solid state interlockings installed from Cannon Street and Hither Green boxes. The box also has a 1995 NX panel, controlling lines beyond the immediate vicinity. Here, in January 2014, Trevor Maxted chats to signaller Phil Price about the operation of the frame.

Waterloo: The central part of the massive 309-lever frame at Waterloo is seen here in 1980. The frame was divided into three parts. The central bank of levers contained 159 levers with two identical smaller panels either side of the main frame, each with 75 levers. The lever frame at Waterloo was replaced by an NX panel in 1984. (Trevor Maxted)

SECTION 3
POWER BOX TO IECC AND RETB – THE ROAD TO ERTMS (EUROPEAN RAILWAY TRAFFIC MANAGEMENT SYSTEM).

For two decades up to the 1980s the NX panel was the most prevalent method of signalling on major lines in the UK. The last large scheme to use this conventional technology was the 1989 Waterloo resignalling when a large NX panel was built at Wimbledon.

The real step change in train control came with the introduction of microprocessor interlocking in the 1980s. This used solid state interlocking as opposed to electromechanical relay interlocking. This may be considered a bit like the change from traditional television with the large tube to flat screen digital TVs. The impact is considerable in that banks of relays which formerly occupied large rooms underneath the signal box can now be housed in small boxes. A box less than 2ft long is all that is needed for the relays to control 40 signals and 40 sets of points.

Added to this are two replicate boxes as a safety feature and then the power, transmission and interlockings. This means that a major station can be controlled from a large filing cabinet packed with equipment as compared to needing the footprint of half a tennis court for traditional relay interlocking.

With digital interlocking came VDU displays to represent the track work and then automation of some functions like route setting and automatic route setting (ARS). The signaller was transformed from the instigator of all moves to the observer of an automated system, ready to intervene should there be problems. Thus the integrated electronic control centre (IECC) was born.

Running at level 2 ETCS, Class 313 No. 313121 races along the Hertford loop on December 15, 2014. Staff from the National Operating Strategy Office rail safety and operating departments benefit from this tour to help understand the radical changes sweeping the network.

Shift manager Andy Harwell keeps a watchful eye on the screens at the IECC in York. Having started life as a signaller at Flaxton, followed by spells as a shunter in York North yards, then a signaller in Tollerton, Thirsk and Leeds, he became a shift manager in Leeds. This position led to him being involved in the transfer of control of the Leeds area into the IECC and then to further strategic roles in the planning of the new ROC. The screens of the IECC are stretched out in front of him, with Leeds station fourth from the left and York seventh. Leeds experiences 1100 movements per day as compared to 400 in York.

AUTOMATIC TRAIN PROTECTION

A second development, integral to ERTMS and dating back to 1894, is automatic train protection (ATP). In the late 1890s the fog man was stationed trackside whenever visibility dropped and there was the risk of a driver passing a signal at danger. His job (for they were invariably men) was to place detonators on the track whenever the distant signal was at 'caution'.

These detonators had to be removed once the signal was set to 'all clear', and replaced again once the train had passed and the signal returned to 'caution'. The work was dangerous and errors were made. In addition, trains without continuous braking often failed to stop in the allotted distance in any case. In this context in 1894, Vincent Raven, the chief engineer on the North Eastern Railway developed a system of trip wires and rods which would trigger a valve on the locomotive if a signal was at danger.

This released steam into a whistle located in the cab, alerting the driver to a signal at caution or danger. The system was so successful it was introduced along the East Coast mainline north of York from 1901 onwards. Further development in 1907 trialled an electrical system with a cab alert which was introduced on several major North Eastern lines.

The Great Western Railway was also developing automatic train protection in the early 20th century. After a major accident at Slough in 1900, the railway developed a protection system based on ramps placed between the rails. These interacted with a 'shoe' under the steam locomotive which electromagnetically released steam into a whistle in the cab, similar in principle to Raven's design on the NER.

The electromagnetic ramp was to prove the simpler and more reliable system and was used unchanged on the GWR until the 1948 Nationalisation. With some modifications to add a visual as well as an audible warning, the GWR system became the British Railways Advanced Warning System (AWS) still in use today. The generic terms for AWS is automatic train protection or ATP.

ERTMS (EUROPEAN RAILWAY TRAFFIC MANAGEMENT SYSTEMS)

What is ERTMS? This is the system that will be the standard throughout Europe to control the railways of the future. It has four key elements:
1. ETCS (European Train Control Systems) – this is basically cab signalling
2. GSM-R (Global System for Mobile Communications – Railways) – this allows communication between the signaller and the train and back the other way.
3. TMS (Traffic Management System) – this is a computer programme that not only runs the normal service but is used to recover the normal service after disruption as fast as possible.
4. EOR (European Operating Rules) – a rulebook designed to be universally accepted in Europe.

All over Europe in the 1980s, the national railway networks were developing their own versions of automatic train protection, none of which were compatible with each other. In 1989, it was in this context that the European Transport Minister asked the European Institute of Railway Research to develop an interoperable system for ATP.

The aim was to produce ERTMS, an international standard programme which would provide a common interoperable platform for railways, traffic control and signalling. In 1993 the ERTMS group was formed by the national railways of Germany, France and Italy (with other EU member states joining later). Thus it was in 1996 that ERTMS was adopted as standard through out Europe. Several other facets of railway operation were also standardised in the 1990s. First the Turnkey project of 1991 set standards for all high speed (200kph+) and high capacity lines in the European Union.

Then GSM-R (Global Systems for Mobile communications for Railways) was introduced as the standard for all railway communications. Finally in 1998, the Union of European Signalling Companies (UNISIG) was formed to standardise technical specifications of signalling equipment throughout the continent.

ERTMS communications manager Jim Lynch explains the onboard hardware needed to allow a train to operate under ERTMS.

The top box contains the GSM-R communication equipment, the next has safety relays. The largest cabinet, just above the orange box, is the heart of ETCS. It contains solid state cards programmed with the unique characteristics of this unit as well as wheel sensors, detectors for the trackside balises... and all in triplicate. The reason for triplicate components is that the train works on the two out of three principle. Thus, two identical boxes must agree exactly and be functioning for the train to operate. This allows a single box to fail (and be replaced at the earliest opportunity), but still means instructions must be duplicated exactly for the train to function.

The orange box at the bottom of the stack is the ETCS recorder. This is not the same as the 'black box' which records what the train and driver has done, but records exactly what signals have been sent to and from the train. In any incident this can be checked to ensure the signalling systems were not at fault. A major problem in modern trains is retrofitting this much equipment to already overcrowded multiple units with small driving cabs. Fitting new rolling stock is not a problem as the need for a small filing cabinet of electronics can be built in at design stage. More difficult is working out where to put everything in a Class 313 EMU commuter train. Luggage space and toilets are two of the suggestions already mooted.

ETCS & TMS

Two of the key elements of ERTMS are Traffic Management System (TMS) and European Train Control System (ETCS). ETCS may be broken down into four levels:

Level 0 is where the train is fitted with ETCS but the infrastructure is not ETCS compatible. This is the current state of affairs on most tracks in the UK with fixed trackside signals, ATP in operation and signals controlled directly from either a manual or power signal box.

Level NTC (National Train Control) is the same as level 0, but ETCS fitted trains have onboard equipment which will read AWS and TPWS, thus offering the same level of protection currently to conventional trains. For this reason, the railways on the UK mainland will not generally adopt level 0.

Level 1 introduces cab signalling equipment which gets it's movement authority from track mounted balises (French for beacon). It retains the trackside infrastructure. Thus cab signalling may be used in newer rolling stock and motive power, but the trackside infrastructure remains for older stock.

Level 2 is where there are no longer trackside signals, but axle counters and track circuits still provide train detection. The Cambrian system, which was originally a Radio Electronic Token Block system is now a level 2 system, controlled from Machynlleth. Here the movement authority is displayed on the driver's in-cab screen (Driver Machine Interface DMI), messages being sent to the train using the GSM-R radio system. On the Cambrian the balises are passive, merely transmitting data when energised by a passing train.

Level 3 – here the movement authority is sent to the train as in level 2, but train detection no longer relies on track circuits and axle counters to establish the exact position. Rather position is determined by GPS, doppler radar situated under the train, and an odometer on the

Running in level 2 ETCS, the driver is observed by a second traction supervisor (who has a monitor to watch the cab signalling) as 313121 heads south on one of six runs along the test track on December 15, 2014.

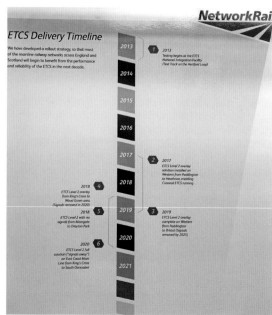

Starting with being introduced on Crossrail in 2017, the new cab signalling system will be rolled out between Paddington and Bristol by 2019 and then between King's Cross and Doncaster by the end of 2020.

The specially fitted unit arrives at Hitchin, at the end of the morning's test runs, and the observers detrain.

train wheels. Data from these three inputs is collated onboard and transmitted to the signalling centre via GSM-R. This use of the GPS system helps overcome problems of wheel slip or temporary speed restrictions, which might see a train lose its expected position between trackside balises by as much as 5%.

Network Rail has invested heavily in equipment and facilities to test all the ETCS systems in production at the moment. Central to this is a converted Class 313 Silverlink EMU No. 313121. This unit has been equipped with cab signalling and is used as a mobile test bed for software and hardware from various manufacturers.

On the day of my visit in December 2014, the unit was testing Siemens equipment. Running along a seven mile stretch of track centred at Watton on Stone, the unit is controlled by a signaller based in ENIF (ERTMS National Integration Facility) in Hitchin goods yard. For the duration of the test, the 'down' line is switched from King's Cross panel box to the control of the test facility in Hitchin.

The illustrations show the unit in action as well as the control centre in Hitchin. As for the introduction of cab signalling and the removal of trackside signals, this will be a gradual process. Network Rail has, however, set a timetable for the introduction of this technology for the lines between Paddington and Bristol by 2019 with Paddington to Heathrow as part of the Crossrail project operational by 2017.

Ewan Spencer from Siemens explains the ENIF testing facility to our party. His colleague is running a simulation of Reading station which has been chosen by Siemens to fit in with other suppliers which have been allocated King's Cross and Paddington. Rolling out ERTMS and ETCS from simple straight track to major stations like Reading is a challenge which might need days of track occupations, disrupting the train service. The investment in ENIF obviates this need and allows the majority of testing to be done in the laboratory, before the system is installed and operated live on the mainline. The ENIF facility has separate testing rooms for all four major manufacturers which will be bidding for work as ERTMS is rolled out across the UK.

TMS

A second element of ERTMS is Traffic Management System (TMS). This system, initially supplied by Thales, is being introduced into the ROCs in Cardiff and Romford at the end of 2015 before being rolled out nationally. This system operates in a similar way to ARS by setting routes automatically according to the timetable.

It is also a problem solving computer programme which looks ahead and addresses potential conflicts before they occur. With input from other sources, including stock and crew diagrams it also has the power to recover the train service following periods of disruption. A trackside incident may cause several hours of disruption and at the moment resolving this sort of problem involves many people in different offices.

The ROC pod concept will place all staff from the signaller, controller and TOC next to each other, but the traffic management will go a step further by offering immediate solutions to restore the service as quickly as possible. The programme factors in known infrastructure limitations, stock availability and staff rosters and offers what it thinks is the quickest way to get things back on track.

Should any member of the team in the pod think they have a better idea, this can be entered and the programme will compute whether the new suggestion speeds up or delays the restoration of a normal service.

SECTION 4
REGIONAL OPERATING CENTRES (ROCS)

Responsibility for the control of the entire UK railway network will rest with 12 rail operating centres, known as ROCs for short. These new 'bunkers', based very much on the control centres of North American Railroads, are as far from the Victorian signal boxes of our current system as the horse and cart is from the TGV.

Initially the drive to develop the ROCs was asset driven because of the large number of manual signal boxes needing repair and renovation, not to mention the 5000 signallers employed in them, costing millions of pounds every year. However, as the ROC projects have developed round the country it is clear that the real benefits are not just in the savings from eliminating labour intensive older assets, but from the performance and capacity improvements that will accrue once signalling and control are merged together in these new centres.

This is because these centres will be responsible for traditional signalling control, but they will also handle traffic management, a responsibility previously based in regional control centres. To understand the make up and function of a ROC, I was invited to visit the York ROC by Network Rail and given a guided tour of the signalling and control centre as well as the York Academy and Training Centre and the York IECC.

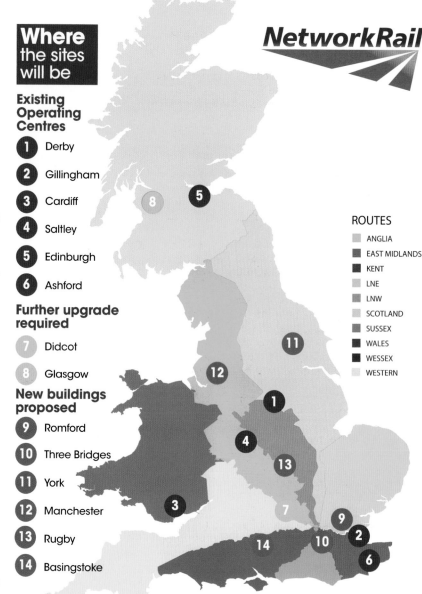

Where the sites will be

Existing Operating Centres

1. Derby
2. Gillingham
3. Cardiff
4. Saltley
5. Edinburgh
6. Ashford

Further upgrade required

7. Didcot
8. Glasgow

New buildings proposed

9. Romford
10. Three Bridges
11. York
12. Manchester
13. Rugby
14. Basingstoke

ROUTES

- ANGLIA
- EAST MIDLANDS
- KENT
- LNE
- LNW
- SCOTLAND
- SUSSEX
- WALES
- WESSEX
- WESTERN

BELOW: The expanse of the first-floor operations room is seen here in November 2014, as fitting out is almost complete. The vast space houses 73 workstations, each equipped with VDU and state-of-the-art blue controllers' chairs. These workstations are grouped strategically in pods to facilitate more efficient working.

These facilities combine to make up the York 'campus'.

York ROC is the largest of the 12 proposed centres and will eventually control the East Coast mainline from King's Cross to the Scottish borders as well as the many secondary lines in Lincolnshire, Yorkshire and Northumberland. Built by BAM, it has cost £38 million and was due to open its doors to the first staff on January 17, 2015.

Eventually there will be over 400 people based in the building which boasts excellent staff facilities including a gym and a prayer room. The commitment to get things right from the start with the new ROCs is quite impressive. The state of the art gym has space for 12 staff at any one time and is run by Nuffield Health who also run the first aid room.

Staff require a health check before they can use the gym which is strictly for ROC employees. The furnishings of the toilets and kitchens are impressive, but it is the first and second floor control rooms which really demonstrate the commitment to excellence in everything to do with the ROC.

The first migration of signallers will be during 2015 and 2016. Until then the only staff in the building are from Network Rail and the train operating companies control departments. Each work station in the building is positioned to best align signallers, controllers and representatives of the train operating companies (TOCs).

On the first floor, because of the concentration required for signallers to handle complex locations like

York ROC Operations Room

Leeds and York station (with 1100 and 400 trains each day respectively), there is a specially sound proofed divider between the control area and the signallers who will occupy the south of the main operating area. The first four 'migrations' will be from The York IECC, Sheffield Power box, the north Lincolnshire lines and the Hull line – hopefully all completed by the end of 2016.

The current York IECC sits in a less than glamorous prefabricated building to the north of the new ROC. Here I met Andy Harwell, the shift manager who started on the railway at Flaxton signal box, before working as a shunter in York North yards, then back to signalling in Tollerton, Thirsk and finally Leeds.

It was the move to work as a manager in Leeds that led to Andy's involvement in the IECC and the ROC. Instrumental in helping incorporate the complex Leeds area into the IECC in York, Andy has also been part of the planning team that has designed the pod concept for the second floor described below.

Back on the first floor, I find that signallers are provided with state of the art 'controller' chairs which cost £1200 apiece. But for those with back or musculoskeletal problems, Network Rail allows specially designed chairs to meet the individual's particular needs. These chairs even have their own cupboard at the south end of the first floor.

Not everything is rosy however as health and safety has caused a stir by refusing to allow staff to use the wonderful south facing balcony, designed for coffee and meal breaks. Health and safety officers have declared it may be risky because a gust of wind from the south could blow in through the patio doors and should a signaller in one of the four migrations be doing paperwork on a SPAD or similar incident, his or her papers might blow off the desk.

Yes this is seriously the state of play during December 2014 – as a neutral observer I just wonder if investing in some shiny Network Rail paperweights might be a cost effective and relatively simple solution. It seems a terrible waste not to use the spacious balcony at the south end of the first floor.

Anyway, when further migration of signallers occurs to the top floor, the seating arrangements will be even more integrated than those on the first floor. The seating will be designed in 'pods' where signaller, controller and TOC staff for a given area will all be adjacent to one another. This may not sound particularly revolutionary, but it is.

In the past signallers have worked, largely in isolation. Control of an area has been handled from offices many miles from the signaller on the front line while staff from the various TOCs operating in an area were housed in yet more distant offices. Whenever an incident or delay occurred, phone lines ran hot and multiple conversations were needed to arrive at a suitable solution.

More recently conference calls have been used to resolve locomotive failures, trackside incidents and other problems. Imagine then that all the relevant decision makers for a given area will now be sitting within touching distance of each other in the ROC. They will get to know each other, understand each other's working environments and limitations.

This is the human side of what is a gradual merger of signalling and traffic management into a single discipline. This evolution of working practices should make rapid decision making in the face of service disruption much easier and be one of the biggest revolutions of the new resignalling of Britain.

One concrete example of this at the new York ROC is the problem in GNER days of trains waiting outside York because their booked platform was occupied. GNER controllers followed GNER policy, which was that platform alterations could not be made less than 20 minutes before the booked arrival of a train because of the disruption to passengers who would need to hurry to change platforms.

Any request from the signaller to divert an arrival to another platform had to be made to the Network Rail controller, the train company controller and finally the station dispatch team and announcer. By the time these people, all in different offices had been contacted, the train had almost invariably come to a standstill outside York anyway.

Now with all parties working within touching distance, it is hoped simple problems like this will be anticipated and solved within a matter of minutes, thus reducing delay. ■

ABOVE: The York ROC, which opened for business in January 2015, stands south of the station and is clad in brick. This is in contrast to the other ROCs where concrete and steel cladding is the order of the day. The historic city of York felt the building should be in keeping with the other historic buildings in the area and so insisted on a brick outer surface.

Next to the York ROC, but within the same building, is the York Academy and Training Centre. As well as extensive facilities to train maintenance staff, there are several classrooms for signallers. As well as IECC and VDU-based training there are three rooms, where training on both NX panels and manual lever frames is available. One of these rooms is seen here with a class in progress. The lever frame used for training is called Hornby Junction.

Wales

CARDIFF ROC

The opening of the South Wales Signalling Centre on the site of the old Canton Goods depot spelt the beginning of the end for manual signalling in Wales. This building will be enlarged and altered to form the ROC responsible for control of all railways in South and North Wales.

In January 2010 the first phase of the new project took over control of the mainline from Patchway to Maindee East Junction, an area formerly controlled by the 1962 vintage Newport panel (the NX panel controlling this part of the South Wales mainline was in fact installed in 1968). In 2011 the remaining half of the Newport panel controlling Maindee East Junction to Marshfield was transferred,

followed by the Vale of Glamorgan line in March 2013.

In September 2013, the Rhymney Valley lines controlled by Bargoed, Ystrad Mynach and Heath Junction signals boxes migrated to the centre and finally in October 2013, the Shrewsbury to Crewe line finally made its belated entry to the ROC.

Before 2010 many manual signal boxes had survived not only in the South Wales Valleys, but also in West and North Wales. Once transfer of control to the Cardiff ROC is mostly complete in 2020, there will have been at least a further 43 manual boxes from Holyhead to Clarbeston Road, closed and relocated to computer screens in the Cardiff 'bunker'.

LEFT: *Bishton*: Bishton signal box is a wonderful anachronism, which according to Network Rail, will not close until 2045! One suspects this might be brought forward as the South Wales mainline is electrified. The box guards a crossing to the east of Llanwern steelworks. It was opened in 1941 and was reduced to the status of a ground frame in 1961, when Newport panel took over control of the four-tracked South Wales mainline. At this stage the 38-lever frame was reduced to just three levers and a further two to control the wicket gates for pedestrians. Here, in 1995, the signalman winds the gate wheel to allow some farm traffic over the South Wales mainline in a scene which defies logic in the 21st century.

RIGHT: *Port Talbot*: The Port Talbot 'power signal box' opened in 1963. The extensive NX panel is seen here during a 1982 impromptu visit. The panel may be the last of the 1960s South Wales modernisation boxes to survive as it is not scheduled to be subsumed by the Cardiff ROC until 2020.

ABOVE: *Barry*: The last-surviving Barry Railway signal box at Barry station closed on June 27, 2014. The box was unusual in that until 1895, the Barry Railway had relied on Saxby and Farmer for its signalling products. The 1897-built box, was in fact constructed by Evans & O'Donnell, and the design owes much to the boxes built by this company on the Great Eastern Railway. Originally it had a 117-lever frame, which was updated to a standard Great Western design in 1957. In the 1970s the frame was shortened to 77 levers. The box is seen here in 1995 as Class 150 No. 150265 departs towards Cardiff with a Merthyr service.

HISTORICAL SCHEMES
RADYR RESIGNALLING AND THE SOUTH WALES VALLEYS

Looking first at the lines north from Newport, even in the late 1970s there were only a few signal boxes left in operation on what, by this stage, were freight-only lines. Leaving the South Wales main line at Gaer Junction, the first manual box was at Park Junction. The only other signal boxes lay on the line to Ebbw Vale steelworks at Lime Kiln Junction and Aberbeeg. Aberbeeg closed in 1997, while it was not until 2007 that the crossing box at Lime Kiln Junction closed (closed May 14, 2007, and demolished June 20, 2007) and all traffic on the Ebbw Vale line was controlled by a newly installed NX panel in Park Junction. Park Junction itself is scheduled to close with its work transferred to the Cardiff ROC in 2017.

Perhaps the first major rationalisation in the South Wales valleys, during the diesel era, came in 1984 when Heath Junction was remodelled to free up land for house building. The old Great Western box was replaced by a temporary building and an NX panel.

The small panel at Heath fringed with the Cardiff power box to the south and Aber box to the north until 1987 when Aber Junction closed (coincident with the closure of the 'big hill' from Aber to Walnut Tree Junction (a coal route allowing coal from the Rhymney Valleys direct access to Radyr yard, avoiding Cardiff).

Then in 2013 the last two boxes in the Rhymney valley at Ystrad Mynach and Bargoed closed, with the temporary building at Heath Junction also closing and all control handed over to the Cardiff ROC.

The Taff Vale lines, north from Radyr diverge at Pontypridd and again at Abercynon. By the 1980s, the Rhondda valley line had just two signal boxes at Gyfeillion Upper (adjacent to Tymawr colliery) and Porth. The small manual box at Porth was unique in that it opened in 1981 with a 16-lever frame and was the last lever box to be opened in the UK.

Gyfeillion Upper box closed on December 16, 1984, while the new Porth box did not close until October 1998 when it was transferred to the Radyr control centre. One valley over on the line to Aberdare, just one signal box remained once the passenger service was reintroduced and this was Abercwmboi.

This closed in 1989 with control of the whole Aberdare branch maintained from Abercynon. The lever box at Abercynon closed in 2008, with a temporary building on the same site housing an NX panel. On the Merthyr line, the last remaining signal box was at Black Lion Colliery and this closed in June 1992.

Further south, the major changes came in 1997 and 1998 when the Radyr signalling centre was opened. This led to the closure of signal boxes at Pontypridd, Maesmawr, Walnut Tree Junction, Radyr Junction, Llandaff Loop and Radyr Quarry Junction. Looking forward it is anticipated that the small signalling panels at Abercynon and Radyr will transfer to the Cardiff ROC in 2017.

Further west there are still several other manual signal boxes in the valleys. Tondu remains open on the branch to Maesteg with a proposed closure date in 2043, although this seems unduly optimistic. Further west is Neath and Brecon Junction signal box, again with a closure date set for 2055. The final manual boxes left on the old valley lines to the South Wales coalfield are at Pantyffynnon and Pantyffynnon South Level crossing and these also have a provisional closure date set for 2045.

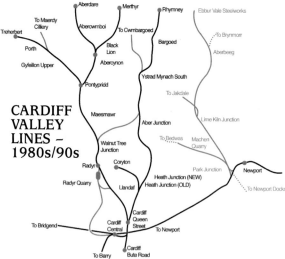

CARDIFF VALLEY LINES – 1980s/90s

YEAR	BOXES TRANSFERRED
2011	Newport PSB
2012	Caldicot, Lydney and second part of Newport PSB
2013	Crewe Bank, Harlescott, Nantwich, Prees, Wem, Whitchurch, Wrenbury, Llanelli West, Bargoed, Cardiff PSB, Aberthaw
2014	Barry, Cowbridge Road
2015	St Fagans, Llanelli West
2016	Abergele, Deganwy, Holywell Junction, Llandudno Junction, Llandudno station, Mostyn, Prestatyn, Rhyl, Rockcliffe Hall, Talacre, Tyn-y-Morfa, Heath Junction, Ystrad Mynach South, Cardiff PSB (second part)
2017	Abercynon, Radyr, Abergavenny, Bromfield, Craven Arms, Dorrington, Hereford, Leominster, Little Mill Junction, Marsh Brook, Moreton-on-Lugg, Onibury, Pontrilas, Tram Inn, Wooferton Junction, Park Junction, Tondu
2018	Bishton
2020	Port Talbot PSB, Bangor, Gaerwen, Holyhead, Llandudno Junction (second part), LlanfairPG, Llanwrst, Penmaenmawr, Ty Croes, Valley, Neath & Brecon Junction, Pantyffynnon & LC, Tal-y-Cafn,
2022	Carmarthen Junction, Clarbeston Road, Ferryside, Kidwelly, Pembrey, Whitland
2025	Abbey Foregate, Dee Marsh Junction, Severn Bridge Junction, Sutton Bridge Junction, Crewe Junction, Gobowen North, Croes Neweydd North, Penyfordd, Machynlleth Signalling Centre
2048	Ledbury

ABOVE: *Lime Kiln Sidings*: In July 1979, Class 37 No. 37158 passes Lime Kiln Sidings signal box, 'engine and van' from Ebbw Junction depot to Celynen South colliery. The box here dated from 1897 and had a 29-lever frame with a mechanical crossing gate wheel. It closed in 2007.

LEFT: *Aberbeeg*: An interior view of the box at Aberbeeg, taken in 1995, just two years before it closed, shows the block token machine for the branch to Ebbw Vale, and the 65-lever frame which, since closure of the branch to Rose Heyworth colliery in 1982 and the subsequent closure of all the sidings here, is mainly white (or disused) levers.

BELOW: *Aber Junction:* In 1978, the extensive layout at Aber Junction is well seen looking north from the signal box. Class No. 37237, passes from the main Rhymney to Cardiff line onto the branch to Walnut Tree Junction, heading back to Radyr yard, having taken empty coal wagons to Bargoed pits. The box was opened in 1953 with 107 levers and controlled the junctions to Walnut Tree, north of Radyr, as well as the lines seen in the left background, to Windsor colliery. The box closed in 1987 as it was merged into the Heath Junction panel and ceased to have relevance after the closure of the Windsor colliery in 1976 and the line to Radyr from its mothballing in 1982.

ABOVE: *Heath Junction:* This view, taken in September 1984 shows Class 37 No. 37288 with an engineering train carrying ballast and track to rebuild Heath Junction, a few hundred yards north of the old junction. This move was made to free up land for housing to the left of the box.

The 77-lever box here utilised gas lamps for illumination right up until it closed in October 1984.

LEFT: Even back in 1979, the signal box at Heath Junction had lost its nameboard and needed a coat of paint (which it never got before closure and demolition in 1984). Here the permanent way gang pose for a photo.

ABOVE: *Ystrad Mynach*: In August 1994, Class 37 Nos. 37894 and 37896 pause to pick up the single line token for the branch to Cwmbargoed opencast loading sidings. They head an empty MGR from Barry, to be loaded with coal for Aberthaw power station. The signal box here is thought to have opened in 1886 and contained 45 levers when this view was taken. It closed in 2013 when it, Bargoed and the Heath Junction panel box were incorporated into the Cardiff ROC.

Radyr Junction: This view is taken from the box at Radyr Junction and shows the extensive yards at Radyr, which boasted more than 50 sidings and were once extremely busy marshalling coal from the Rhondda, Taff and Rhymney valleys. This 1982 view shows Class 08 No. 08351 arriving from the south with 9E76, the daily trip, with freight from Ferry Road Sidings near Penarth.

Radyr Quarry: In 1990 Radyr yard was a Speedlink Coal hub and here Class 08 No. 08654 shunts HEA hoppers from Abercwmboi Phurnacite plant for domestic depots round the country. Diesel multiple unit Nos. 54273 and 51419 pass the Radyr Quarry box with a Radyr to Coryton 'City Line' train. These services take a full circle of Cardiff and but for the failure to complete the Coryton line to Radyr and Taffs Well in the 19th century would be able to make a full circle of the Welsh capital. Radyr Quarry box was built in 1899 and had 61 levers. It closed in 1998 as part of the Radyr resignalling scheme.

Radyr Junction: The 1961-built Radyr Junction box is seen here in 1977. The original Radyr Junction box had been equipped with 130 levers, but this newer box had just 107. It survived until 1998 when the Radyr SCC took over this area. Here, on a sunny afternoon, Class 37 No. 37227 is held on the Up main line, waiting to cross into the yard, having returned from the valleys as 'engine and van'. An afternoon Barry Island to Merthyr service, packed with commuters passes on the Down mainline.

Abercynon: In this view from February 1999, the box at Abercynon has recently been repainted. Class 66 No. 66026 accelerates north, having just taken the token for the single line section at Aberdare. The train is an empty MGR bound for the newly reopened Tower colliery, where it will load with coal for Aberthaw power station.

Walnut Tree Junction: In November 1977 an unidentified Class 37 curves off the big hill at Walnut Tree Junction, with the afternoon trip from Bargoed Pits to Radyr yard. Using this route from Aber Junction allowed coal trains to avoid the centre of Cardiff on their way to Radyr yard or Aberthaw. Traffic had dropped considerably from the early 1970s levels, however, and from June 1982 the lines from Aber were subject to a trial closure which sadly became permanent. The striking box at Walnut Tree Junction was opened some time after 1908 by the Taff Vale Railway and had 79 levers. It closed in 1998.

LEFT: *Park Junction*:
The signal box at Park Junction has seen many changes in its 129-year lifetime. Built in 1885 it has a 100-lever frame, installed in 1920, but with spaces on the original frame from levers 86-100. In 2007 when the crossing box at Lime Kiln was closed, the NX panel in the corner of the box took over control of the line from Rogerstone to Newbridge. This view, taken in June 1982, shows Class 37 No. 37227 with the 6A77 trip from East Usk yard to Trethomas and Bedwas. The train is crossing over onto the Machen and Bedwas branch, which used to run through to Caerphilly.

ABOVE: *Rhondda Fach South Junction & Porth*: In the summer of 1981, the old Rhondda Fach South Junction signal box, with its 75-lever frame, is still standing. The new ballast has been laid during the spring of 1981, when the layout at Porth was remodelled. In the foreground on the right is the new Porth signal box with its 16-lever frame. This inconspicuous little cabin is a record breaker, in that it was the last lever frame to be opened on British Railways. It closed in 1998 when control of all the Taff Vale lines was transferred to the new Radyr signalling centre.

LEFT: *Pontypridd*: The large box here was opened in 1901 and at the time of this photo in February 1977, had 70 levers. It had, however, been originally 135 levers but the frame had been shortened during rationalisation in 1970. Here, D1010 passes, just two weeks before the end for the Westerns with the Western Requiem rail tour.

Abercwmboi: In 1983, the driver of Class 37 No. 37225 passes the box at the Abercwmboi Phurnacite plant, taking the token for the single line section to Abercynon, with the 09.30 trip to Radyr yard. The box here had 38 levers, opened in 1884 and was rebuilt in 1954, surviving until 1989 when the Phurnacite plant closed and its work was transferred to Abercynon. It was always dirty because of the pollution from the Phurnacite plant.

Abercynon: The 1932 box at Abercynon is seen here in 1994. It has a 34-lever frame and in the background is the NX panel that controls the tracks to Merthyr. As can be seen from the size of the box, there was originally a much larger lever frame, with 93 levers, but incorporation of Stormstown box in 1977 and then the whole Merthyr line in 1989-92 led to a reduced frame and part of the box making space for a panel. My records from this 1994 visit are not as clear as they should be, but I think the signalman was Mr J Morgan from Cwmbach.

Aberbeeg: With a bonfire adding to the atmosphere of dereliction, the driver of Class 37 No. 37293 accepts the single line token for the section to Waunlwyd yard in Ebbw Vale. The train is the 6B92, Cardiff Tidal Sidings to Waunlwyd railfreight metals service, and is captured in July 1988, by which time Severn Tunnel Junction yard had closed and much wagonload traffic was handled in Cardiff Tidal Sidings. The box at Aberbeeg controlled the junction between the Ebbw Vale and Brynmawr branches as well as access to the extensive sidings that used to be here. The box was 1892 and had a 65-lever frame in its heyday. The derelict land behind and to the left of the signal box was where the yard used to be.

THE 'ASSEMBLY' LINE

Rail transport in Wales is basically made up of two main lines in the north and south, with the rural branch line to Aberystwyth across the middle of the country and then the Marches line from Newport to Shrewsbury and Chester, which dips in and out of Wales, but is in England for much of its length. With the establishment of a Welsh Assembly, moves were made to tie together these disparate routes with a Wales centred service from Holyhead to Cardiff.

This was not a natural route for travellers as traffic from North Wales has always flowed east to Liverpool and Manchester or via Crewe to London Euston. Similarly traffic in South Wales is focused on the capital, Cardiff with London-bound passengers travelling to Paddington. Nonetheless, the political imperative was to have a train service tying the disparate halves of the Welsh rail network together and the Welsh Assembly decided to subsidise a new express service between Holyhead and Cardiff. In 2014 there were eight trains each way between Holyhead and Cardiff. While most of the services utilise Class 158 diesel multiple units, one train each way, known as the 'WAG express' or Welsh Assembly Government Express is made up of traditional carriages making the journey in five hours, all subsidised by the Welsh Assembly and relatively lightly loaded (based on personal observations on over a dozen occasions).

One unique element to this journey, now made easy by Welsh government is that the trains are almost totally controlled by manual signal boxes on this route with an amazing 32 boxes along the route from Holyhead to Little Mill where control is handed over to the Cardiff ROC. This section will take the reader on a journey from Holyhead to Little Mill, illustrating each of these structures.

Holyhead: In October 2013, Bangor relief signaller D R Jones checks his box book on a traditional desk as a London service is offered by the station staff. The signal box at Holyhead is an LMS design, dating from 1937. It contains 100 levers, numbered from 16 to 115, as this image clearly shows. The reason for this anomaly is that in 1968 levers 1-15 were removed to provide equipment for the Holyhead Freightliner terminal ground frame. Then, in 1974, the frame in the Holyhead box was extended with the addition of levers 101-115.

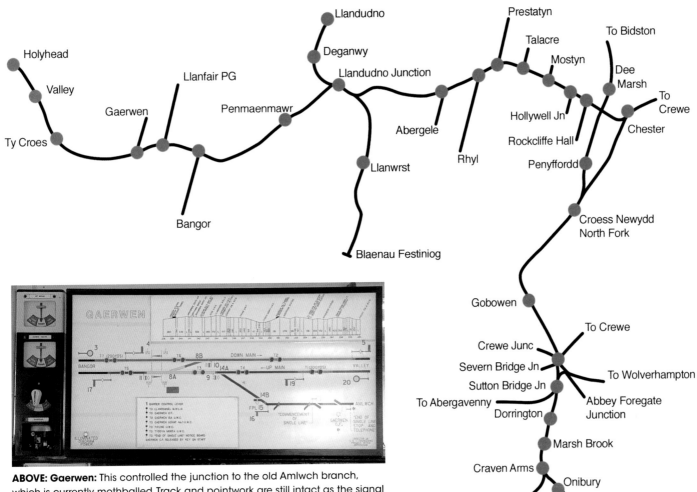

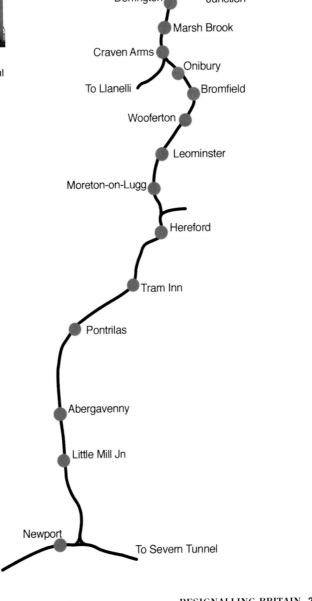

Holyhead

Valley

Ty Croes

Gaerwen

Llanfair PG

Penmaenmawr

Bangor

Llandudno

Deganwy

Llandudno Junction

Abergele

Llanwrst

Rhyl

Blaenau Festiniog

Prestatyn

Talacre

Mostyn

Hollywell Jn

Rockcliffe Hall

Penyffordd

Dee Marsh

To Bidston

To Crewe

Chester

Croess Newydd North Fork

Gobowen

Crewe Junc

Severn Bridge Jn

Sutton Bridge Jn

To Abergavenny

Dorrington

Marsh Brook

Craven Arms

To Llanelli

Onibury

Bromfield

Wooferton

Leominster

Moreton-on-Lugg

Hereford

Tram Inn

Pontrilas

Abergavenny

Little Mill Jn

Newport

To Cardiff

To Severn Tunnel

To Crewe

To Wolverhampton

Abbey Foregate Junction

ABOVE: Gaerwen: This controlled the junction to the old Amlwch branch, which is currently mothballed. Track and pointwork are still intact as the signal diagram shows. The box here dates from 1882 and has 20 levers.

LEFT: *Tram Inn*: The autumn 'rail head treatment train' or RHTT passes Tram Inn on October 30, 2013, headed by Class 66 No. 66126. The circuitous route of the train from Bristol to Cardiff to Ebbw Vale and on to Hereford, before returning to Bristol and Weston-super-Mare, is not dissimilar to the careers of many signallers on today's railway. David Horan, who was at Tram Inn on the day of my visit, left Lancashire in 1992 to work for the railways and, in particular, Welsh Freight. He started as a signaller at Lime Kiln Junction before moving to Little Mill and then to Park Junction in Newport around the time the new panel was installed there to control the Ebbw Vale line. Most recently he took up a post at Tram Inn. The box here was built in 1894 on the footings of an earlier 1880 construction. The 23-lever frame in the box is much more modern, dating from 1978.

ABOVE: *Llandudno Junction*: While Llandudno Junction has been controlled by an NX panel installed in a new signal box, built roughly where the corrugated iron lamp-man's shack is in this 1978 view, it seemed important to include a picture of the original Llandudno Junction box in this section. Originally called Llandudno Junction No.2 (the crudely painted out No.2 can be seen on the box name board), this imposing structure was built in 1898 to the LNWR Type 4 design. Originally it had 118 levers, but was extended to 154 levers in 1921. The No.2 part of the name was dropped in May of 1968 when No.1 box (at the other end of the station) was closed and signalling concentrated here in the old No.2 box. The frame was reduced to 109 levers at the same time. It closed in February 1985 when the new panel box took over. This view, from summer 1978, shows a Metro-Cammel DMU entering the station with a Llandudno to Manchester service.

RIGHT: *Croes Newydd*: The boxes at Croes Newydd used to control the connections between the old Great Western main line to Birkenhead and Brymbo steel works, which closed from October 1982, although the steelworks at Brymbo continued to make steel in small quantities until final closure in 1990. Here, in 1983, Class 47 No. 47340 passes Croes Newydd (North Fork) with the daily Bersham colliery to Fiddlers Ferry power station MGR service. The box was built to a GWR design in 1905, and after extension in 1940 had an 83-lever frame. In 2009 the manual levers were replaced by an NX panel and the box was refurbished with uPVC windows etc.

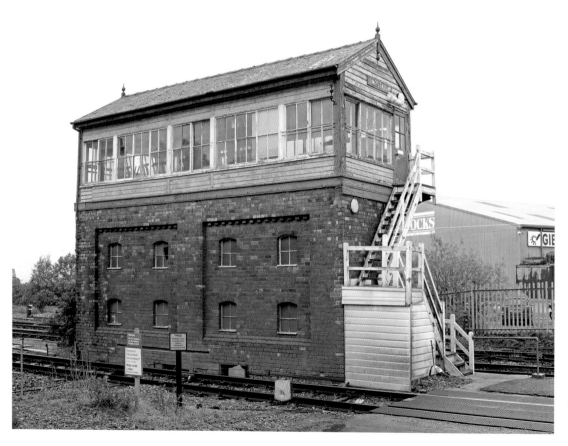

LEFT: *Mostyn*: The 1902 vintage LNWR-design box at Mostyn is seen here in 2012. The box contains a 40-lever frame, but is usually 'switched out' with trains handed straight from Talacre to Holywell Junction.

LEFT: *Holywell Junction*: A Holyhead to Euston express passes Holywell Junction in 2012. In spite of the pouring rain the ships in Mostyn harbour awaiting demolition can still be seen. The box here dates back to 1902 and contains a 54-lever frame. It was modernised in 2004 when uPVC windows were fitted and is due to be closed in 2015. It passes trains on to Rockcliffe Hall signal box, which is of similar construction, and is the only signal box along the 'Assembly Line' not illustrated in this feature.

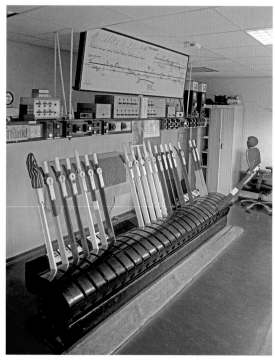

Penmaenmawr. Built in 1952 to a standard BR (LMR) design – which evolved in the 1940s because of worries about bombing raids during the Second World War – Penmaenmawr is perhaps the least sympathetically modernised box on the entire network. The window area was replaced by metal panels in the 1990s giving the box the feel of a bunker or air-raid shelter. Inside, however, is a pristine 20-lever LMR standard frame.

LEFT: *Sutton Bridge*: Sutton Bridge signal box, just south of Shrewsbury, controls the junction to the Aberystwyth line. It used to also control access to the Buildwas and Bewdley branch, which closed in 1963. The box was built in 1913 and contains a 61-lever frame. Here, in 2014, Class 66 No. 66066 passes with an early-morning Margam to Dee Marsh steel train.

ABOVE: *Valley*: The first box out from Holyhead is at Valley. Here, a 1904 LNW signal box controls a level crossing and fringes with Holyhead and Ty Croes. It has 25 levers and was looking a bit worse for wear at the time of my visit in 2013.

LEFT: *Ty Croes*: The 1W93, Cardiff to Holyhead service speeds past Ty Croes box on October 2, 2013. The box is one of the oldest in the UK, dating back to 1872. The lever frame is more modern, dating from 1901, but now reduced from its original 18 levers to just six.

Rhyl: Traffic passing through Rhyl is now controlled by what was Rhyl No.1 box, to the east of the station. Built in 1900 it was refurbished with timber windows in 2007. Here, Mark Pendlebury is seen at the booking desk, with the 90-lever frame behind him. Rhyl No.2 box to the west of the station was also built in 1900 and was larger with a 126-lever frame. It closed in 1990 when Rhyl was rationalised, but has been listed, preventing its demolition. This view shows Class 158 No. 158827 passing with 1D93, a Manchester to Llandudno service. The box is rapidly being overrun by creepers and has had little done to keep it in good condition over the last two decades.

Talacre: On a dreary day in May 2012, Class 175 No. 175108 passes Talacre signal box with the 1G50 Holyhead to Birmingham International service. The signal box here used to control access to Point of Ayr colliery and was built in 1903 to an LNW design. It contains a 24-lever frame which originally operated in Gronant signal box, until re-modelling to fit in Talacre in 1984.

Dorrington: Class 175 No. 175002 passes Dorrington signal box on October 29, 2013. The signal box dates back to 1872 and was of a joint design used by the LNW and GW railways along this line. The 33-lever frame is much more recent, dating from 1941.

Gobowen: The remaining signal box at Gobowen was formerly Gobowen North, but once the coal depot at the south end of the station closed, the connections to the sidings there were worked by a ground frame. The box, seen here in 2012, dates from 1884 and has a 16-lever frame.

ABOVE: Bangor. The box at Bangor was extensively modernised in 2009 with the UPVC windows particularly prominent. It was formerly Bangor No.2 signal box and dates from 1923, built to an LNWR Type 5 design. The 60-lever frame is smaller than the original frame, which boasted approaching 100 levers.

LEFT: Shrewsbury: The four signal boxes in Shrewsbury are remarkable survivors whose future is largely secure due to Grade II listing. The second largest of the boxes is Shrewsbury Crewe Junction, seen here on the right. This 120-lever box was built in 1903 to LNW design and actually has as many active levers today as the much larger Severn Bridge Junction signal box. Shrewsbury is remarkable in that it boasts a mixture of ex-Great Western lower quadrant signals and ex-LNW upper quadrant semaphores. Two of the boxes in the city were ex-LNW, that at Crewe Junction and the now closed Crewe Bank box (shut down as part of the 2013/14 Crewe to Shrewsbury resignalling). Here, on September 29, 2014, Class 66 No. 66620 winds into Coton Hill yard with a Bardon Hill Quarry to Coton Hill yard empty stone train. Later that evening the train went forward as a Coton Hill to Tinsle working – anybody would think that somebody in Freightliner control was 'playing trains'.

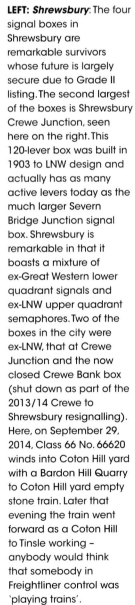

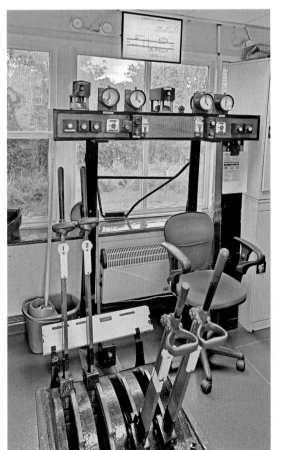

LEFT: Llanfair PG: Not only is this the oldest box along this route (and one of the oldest in the UK) but it boasts the longest name – shortened to Llanfair PG otherwise the name board would be too long to fit on the cabin! The box itself was built in 1871 and contains a four-lever frame which controls the level crossing and dates from 1883. The reduced frame is seen together with the block shelf and signal diagram, viewed in October 2013.

RIGHT: *Shrewsbury*:
The sheer size and scale of the world's largest manual signal box is seen here from the ramparts of Shrewsbury castle. Taken on July 22, 2006, when the temperature in Shrewsbury was 38°C, this shows Class 66 No. 66617 passing with a Saturdays-only Liverpool Docks to Cardiff Tidal Sidings scrap train (for the Allied Steel and Wire works in Cardiff). The box was built in 1903 to an LNW design and has 180 levers. It became the world's largest manual signal box in 2008 when Melbourne Spencer Street, with 191 levers, closed. There have, of course, been larger boxes in the UK, with York Locomotive yard, closed in 1951, having 295 levers and the biggest of them all at Glasgow Central where the Westinghouse miniature lever frame was the biggest ever with 374 levers.

ABOVE: *Shrewsbury*:
With 273 levers on view, this image was taken on April 16, 2012 and shows Class 170 No. 170511 arriving in Shrewsbury with 1J19 the Birmingham International to Aberystwyth and Pwllheli service. Shrewsbury Abbey Foregate box in the foreground, was built in 1914 to a GW design and contains 93 levers.

LEFT: **Pontrilas**: The picture-perfect signal box at Pontrilas dates back to 1880 and contains a 42-lever frame that controls not only the main line but also the siding here, which once loaded timber. As Dan Booth, the signaller on duty tells me, the box was sympathetically renovated in 2009 to cut out the many draughts through the old wooden windows. Here, Class 56 No. 56094 passes with empty timber wagons from Chirk to Briton Ferry, where they will be loaded with logs for the chipboard factory at Chirk.

Onibury: This view, taken from the crossing box at Onibury, shows Class 47 No. 47096 passing with the 00.50 Mossend to Severn Tunnel Junction Speedlink in January 1981. Traffic is the typical mix of steel, chemicals and china clay. The signal box here contains a tiny IFS panel installed when the box was rebuilt in 1977; it controls just two signals.

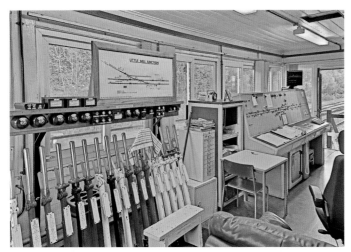

Little Mill Junction: This 1883 Mackenzie and Holland box contains both a manual lever frame with 17 levers, dating from 1938, which controls the Glascoed branch (mothballed some years ago) and an NX panel. The NX panel was installed in 1979 when the Panteg area was rationalised and resignalled and fringed with the power box in Newport until that was taken over by the Cardiff ROC in 2012.

Bromfield: My visit to Bromfield signal box, just north of Ludlow station, was fortunate to coincide with the regular weekly inspection by local operations manager Ian Rowson. The signaller on duty was the brother of Les Bowen from Craven Arms and he was training a new member of staff made redundant when Prees signal box closed as part of the Crewe to Shrewsbury resignalling. The 1873 vintage box is kept in immaculate condition, with the old box totem proudly displayed above the 29-lever frame dating from 1956.

Abergavenny: The 52-lever frame at Abergavenny is seen here in October 2013 as Rob Blackmore looks up some old photographs on the computer. Rob was an area manager before deciding to return as a resident signaller to Abergavenny some years ago. He also recognised me from my South Wales books, published back in the 1980s, when Rob first became interested in railways and chose a career with British Rail. I could have stayed all day chatting in the spacious 1934 GW box, were it not for the fact that there were more boxes needed visiting for this project!

Leominster: Class 47 No. 47148 passes the LNW/GW Joint box at Leominster in May 1985 with 6M44, the Margam to Dee Marsh steel train. The box here dates from 1875 and used to be called Leominster South. It contains a 30-lever frame, which is more modern and dates from 1941.

Hereford: The sun sets over Hereford box in October 2013, catching the forehead of resident signaller Richard Jones. The signal box dates from 1884 and is of LNW/GW design. The frame was reduced from 69 to 60 levers in 1973 and an OCS panel was added to the box in 1984 to control the Shelwick Junction area. Gavin Fry, the local operations manager, explained during my visit that some traditions are alive and well in Hereford in that just like water used to be delivered to Blea Moor signal box by the first freight of the day, so the newspaper is dropped off at the box by the first southbound passenger train of the day!

Abergele: The 1902 LNWR box at Abergele stands between the main running lines. The sympathetically restored box contains a 60 lever frame, but the windows are not quite original as they have been reconstructed to support double glazing. Seen here in October 2013, Class 175 No. 175106 speeds past with 1D32 a Manchester Piccadilly to Holyhead service.

Marshbrook: The LNW/GW Joint line along the Welsh Marches was one of the first in the country to be interlocked in the early 1870s. Five of the distinctive signal boxes built at that time survive and the best preserved of these is Marshbrook which dates from 1872 and has an 18-lever frame. Here, in October 2013, signaller Barry Cank is learning the box from one of the residents, hence two men in such a small signal box.

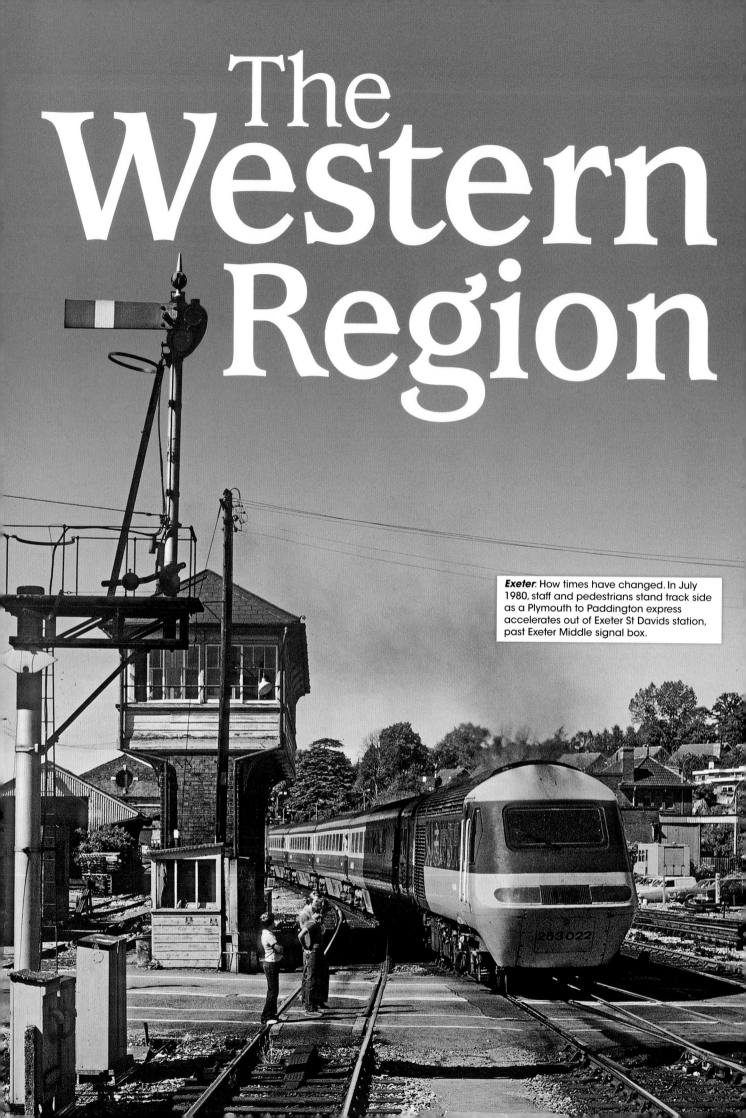

The Western Region

Exeter. How times have changed. In July 1980, staff and pedestrians stand track side as a Plymouth to Paddington express accelerates out of Exeter St Davids station, past Exeter Middle signal box.

DIDCOT ROC

The building used for the Didcot ROC started life as the Thames Valley signalling centre. Opened in 2010, this building will be enlarged to control the whole of the Western Region from Paddington to Penzance. The first signalling stations in the centre opened in March 2010 controlling the line from Reading to Bedwyn. Later in 2010 Reading station itself and the line to Twyford transferred to the centre. In 2011 control of Paddington and the line between there and Twyford migrated to the centre and then in 2012, Didcot itself came under the control of the ROC. To the south the ROC will border the Basingstoke ROC while in the West it will interface with both the Cardiff ROC and the Rugby ROC.

YEAR	BOXES TRANSFERRED
2011	Slough panel
2012	Causeway, Swindon panel
2013	Colthrop, Kintbury
2014	Swindon panel (second part), Minety LC
2015	Gloucester PSB, Bristol PSB, Puxton & Worle, Oxford panel
2017	Slough (second part)
2018	Greenford
2019	Goonbarrow Junction, Liskeard, Lostwithiel, Par, Penzance, Roskear Junction, St Blazey, St Erth, Truro
2021	Alston, St Marys
2022	Plymouth PSB
2025	St Andrews Junction
2026	Crediton, Exeter PSB, Paignton, Oxford (second part), Westbury panel

Exeter. By September 1984 when this picture was taken, a number of new colour light signals were already in place at Exeter St Davids. Class 08 No. 08840 passes the 131-lever Exeter West signal box, framed carefully to exclude the new colour light gantry at the west of the station.

Newton Abbot: The 153-lever Newton Abbot West box is on the left of this view which shows a Paddington to Penzance express leaving Newton Abbot station on July 29, 1985. On the right of the image some of the semaphores controlled by the larger 206-levered East box can be seen, behind a stopping service to Paignton.

SIGNAL BOX	DATE BUILT	DATE CLOSED	NUMBER OF LEVERS
Aller Junction	1925	26/4/1987	46
Athelney	1906	7/4/1986	37
Cogload Junction	1906	7/4/1986	23
Cowley Bridge	1894	29/3/1985	44
Dainton Tunnel	1965	4/5/1987	21
Dawlish Warren	1911	17/11/1986	58
Exeter City Basin	1962	17/11/1986	27
Exeter Middle	1912	29/3/1985	105
Exeter West	1913	3/5/1985	131
Exminster	1924	17/11/1986	80
Newton Abbot East	1926	4/5/1987	206
Newton Abbot West	1927	4/5/87	153
Silk Mill Crossing	1940	23/3/87	53
Taunton East	1931	23/3/1987	147
Taunton West	1931	12/5/1986	135
Teignmouth	1896	17/11/1986	31
Tiverton Junction	1932	1/3/1986	57
Torre	1921	5/10/1986	42
Totnes	1923	8/11/1987	111
Wellington	1931	1/3/1986	50
Whiteball Siding	1955	1/3/1986	27

HISTORICAL SCHEMES
TAUNTON-PLYMOUTH

The Great Western semaphore signalling between Taunton and Plymouth survived well into the 1980s. It's demise started in April 1985 with the commissioning of Exeter power signal box. This led to the closure of Exeter Middle and West signal boxes as well as Cowley Bridge Junction. By th`e completion of the scheme at the end of 1987, a further 18 manual boxes had closed. These included the largest remaining lever frame in the UK at Newton Abbot East with 206 levers and six other manual boxes with over 100 levers. In all the Exeter panel box replaced a total of well over 1500 manual levers! The table below lists the boxes and their closure dates and this section illustrates some of the boxes along this stretch of line.

BELOW: _Taunton_: This busy scene to the east of Taunton station (taken in 1985) shows Class 33 No. 33034 with an Exeter to Bristol stopping service, while Class 47 No. 47373 is awaiting the road from the goods avoiding lines with a lengthy 6C39, St Blazey to Severn Tunnel Junction Speedlink service. To the right of the freight is the 1931-built, 147-levered, Taunton East Junction signal box, which closed in March 1987.

LEFT: *Taunton*: In summer 1980, HST No. 253031 arrives at Taunton from the west with a Plymouth to Paddington express. To the right of the train is Taunton west signal box, built in 1931 and containing 135 levers. This box closed in May 1986.

RIGHT: *Taunton:* A second view at the eastern end of Taunton station, this time taken on July 29, 1985, illustrates the fine GW bracket signals protecting access to Taunton station. Class 45 No. 45108 passes with a Newcastle to Plymouth cross country express.

Goonbarrow Junction: Goonbarrow Junction signal box is one of the least accessible on the network, situated as it is within the European China Clay factory in the village of Bugle. Seen here on a foggy morning in 2012, the brick-built GW box dates from 1909 and contains 25 levers.

FEATURED LINES
LISKEARD-PENZANCE

By far the largest number of traditional manual signal boxes to remain in the area to be controlled by Didcot ROC are in Cornwall. The transfer of these boxes to the Didcot ROC is not scheduled until 2019, giving plenty of time to visit the area and see traditional Victorian signalling in action.

LEFT: *Liskeard*: Liskeard signal box fringes with the power box in Plymouth and controls the junction between the West of England mainline and the Looe branch. Built in 1915 of wooden construction, it contains 36 levers.

LEFT & BELOW: *Lostwithiel*: On April 9, 2013, HST No. 43005 brings up the rear of a late-running Paddington to Penzance express as it leaves Lostwithiel station. The signal box dates back to 1893 and as well as a 63-lever manual frame which controls the junction with the Fowey branch, there is a small NX panel in the box. This was installed in December 1991 and is a Westinghouse design, which controls the mainline to Par. Although new uPVC windows have been fitted they are moderately sympathetic to the original timber frames.

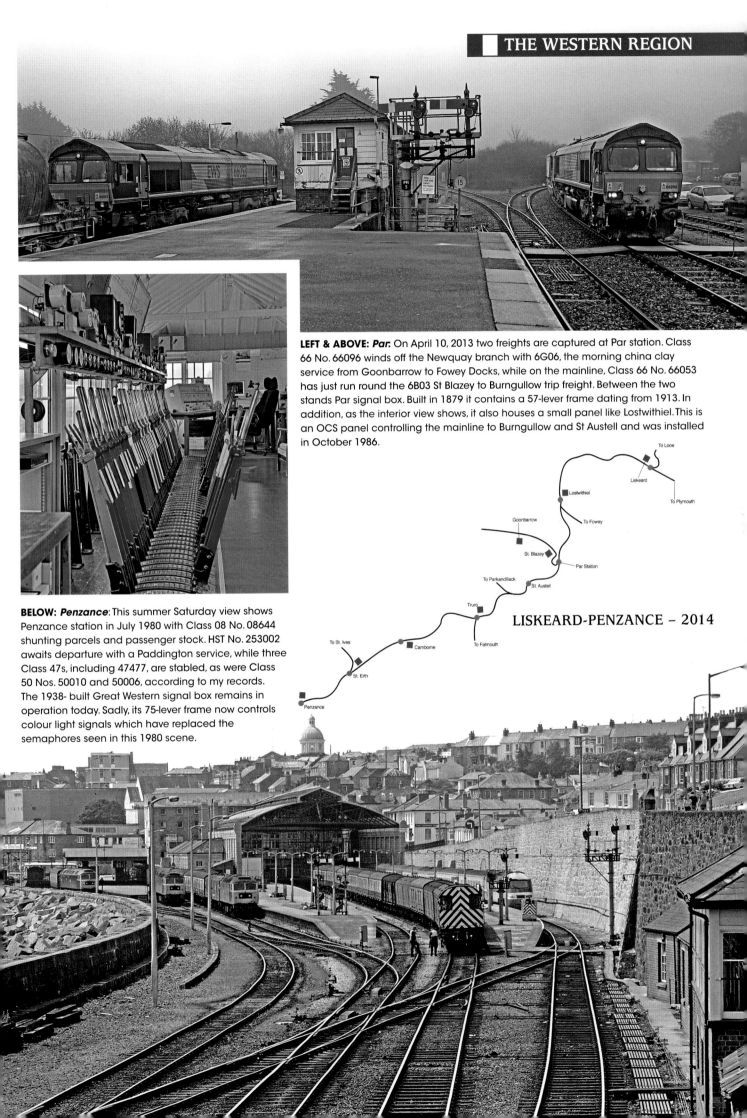

LEFT & ABOVE: *Par:* On April 10, 2013 two freights are captured at Par station. Class 66 No. 66096 winds off the Newquay branch with 6G06, the morning china clay service from Goonbarrow to Fowey Docks, while on the mainline, Class 66 No. 66053 has just run round the 6B03 St Blazey to Burngullow trip freight. Between the two stands Par signal box. Built in 1879 it contains a 57-lever frame dating from 1913. In addition, as the interior view shows, it also houses a small panel like Lostwithiel. This is an OCS panel controlling the mainline to Burngullow and St Austell and was installed in October 1986.

BELOW: *Penzance*: This summer Saturday view shows Penzance station in July 1980 with Class 08 No. 08644 shunting parcels and passenger stock. HST No. 253002 awaits departure with a Paddington service, while three Class 47s, including 47477, are stabled, as were Class 50 Nos. 50010 and 50006, according to my records. The 1938- built Great Western signal box remains in operation today. Sadly, its 75-lever frame now controls colour light signals which have replaced the semaphores seen in this 1980 scene.

LISKEARD-PENZANCE – 2014

To Looe
Liskeard
Lostwithiel
To Plymouth
Goonbarrow
To Fowey
St. Blazey
Par Station
To Parkandillack
St. Austell
Truro
To St. Ives
Camborne
To Falmouth
St. Erth
Penzance

RIGHT: *St Erth*: In July 1983 a local service from Plymouth to Penzance arrives at St Erth behind Class 50 No. 50041. The signal box here dates from 1899 and contains a 69-lever frame which controls the mainline and the junction with the St Ives branch.

RIGHT: *St Blazey*: On an unusually dull day in July 1980, Class 46 No. 46020 accelerates out of St Blazey yard with the daily St Blazey to Acton fitted freight. To the left of the signal box are the old vacuum-braked china clay hood wagons, used for traffic to Par Harbour and Fowey Docks. The Acton freight itself contained VIX ferry wagons from Goonbarrow to Zeebrugge via the Harwich train ferry, carrying china clay. There were also ferry vans from Par Harbour to Mannheim, Gluckstadt and Basle via Harwich. Finally, the train had some VWV vans with china clay from St Blazey to shed B at King's Dock in Swansea, the consignee for which was Clan Graham. My unusually detailed records are almost certainly the result of Paul Shannon exhorting me to record the consists of freights around this time.

ABOVE & RIGHT:
St Blazey: On April 9, 2013, Class 66 No. 66096 winds past St Blazey signal box, passing through the long-abandoned passenger station. It is working 6G08, the afternoon Goonbarrow to Fowey china clay train, and just out of shot to the right of this view, the driver will surrender the single line token. In the interior view, taken minutes later, the single line token can be seen hanging on its hook at the end of the box. Built in 1908, the box has a 41-lever frame, which is predicted to continue in operation (like the rest of the Cornish boxes) until 2019 when it will transfer to the Didcot ROC.

LEFT: *Truro*: On July 28, 1982, a summer 'extra' stopping service from Plymouth to Penzance arrives in Truro. The train is made up of 10 Mk1 carriages, and my records suggest it was packed (standing room only). Class 50 No. 50037 is passing Truro signal box (formerly Truro East). This cabin was built in 1899 and contains a 54-lever frame, which was installed as late as 1971 when it was reclaimed after closure of boxes in the Bristol area as a result of the opening of the Bristol power signal box in March 1970.

West Midlands

Dunhampstead: The signal man with carpet strapped to his shoes to avoid marking the floor is probably a sign of the times at Dunhampstead. The box was reduced to a crossing box back in March 1969, but still functioned with a three-man shift in 1985 when this image was taken. Built in 1902 to a Midland Railway design, it originally had 16 levers, but was just a crossing box with two working levers when this image was taken in 1985. The box closed altogether in July 1986 when the crossing here was converted to Automatic Half Barriers, controlled from the Gloucester Panel Box. A sad episode, as the nearby pub served great beer and cider as well as good food, and there was time to leap up from the pub garden to photograph passing trains.

LEFT: *Malvern Wells*: Class 50 No. 50007 named *Sir Edward Elgar* passes Malvern Wells signal box with the 16.00 Hereford to Paddington express. The box here dates from 1919 and contains a 40-lever frame.

THE WEST MIDLANDS ROCS – SALTLEY AND RUGBY

Originally control of the rail network in the West Midlands was to be handled at the Saltley Signalling Control Centre. This was constructed as part of the West Coast Mainline Passenger Control Upgrade which envisaged 140mph running between Euston and the North West.

The scheme was never implemented, but Saltley Control Centre was built as a robust, bombproof building, fit for controlling the high speed-railway that had been planned.

Opened in 2007, the first old panel box to be moved to Saltley was Coventry, followed by North Warwick and Snow Hill in 2008. After Oxley in 2010, Water Orton was added in 2011 and then Stourbridge in 2012. In 2013 Walsall and Bescot were added with the notable closure of Bescot Down yard signal box which had been suggested for listing by English Heritage. Sadly February 2014 saw the old hump panel box demolished.

There is however no room to accommodate a fully functioning ROC in the Saltley building and it is therefore envisaged that once the West Midlands has been fully moved to control in Saltley, there will be a business case to move the whole signalling and traffic management operation to the ROC in Rugby. Moving the hardware from Saltley (the solid state interlockings etc.) would be very expensive. A more realistic solution is to leave the interlockings in the building at Saltley and install a remote interface to control them from the ROC in Rugby.

The Rugby ROC interfaces with Manchester to the north and Cardiff ROC to the West. To the south are the ROCs at Didcot and Basingstoke, while the eastern border of much of the area controlled by Rugby is under the Derby ROC.

Saltley ROC also known as West Midlands Signalling Centre (NB it is anticipated that this ROC will be merged into the Rugby ROC in 2018)

BELOW: *Henwick*: Dating back as far as 1875, but modernised in 1897, Henwick is one of the oldest signal boxes on the network. Here, in 1985, a Hereford to Birmingham New Street has just passed in the form of an ex-Paddington suburban diesel multiple unit. The box has 25 levers and controls the signals at Worcester Foregate Street Station on the other side of the River Severn.

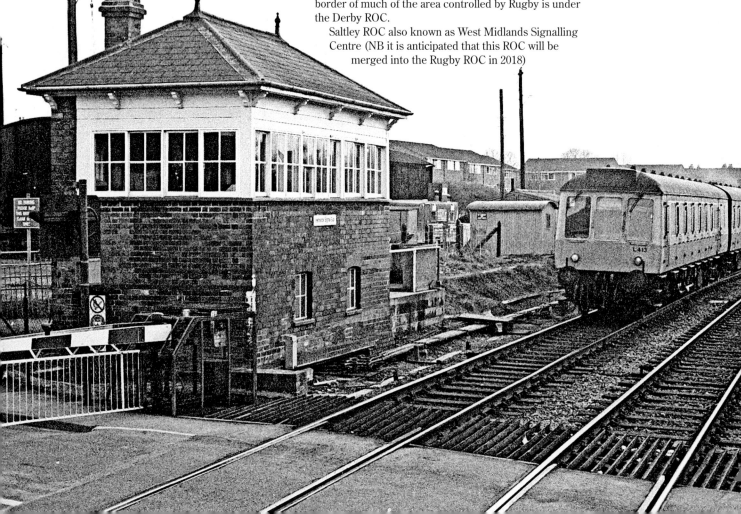

Droitwich Spa: On May 30, 1985, Class 45 No. 45020 passes Droitwich Spa signal box with 6V70, the daily Cliffe Vale to St Blazey china clay is of classic GW brick-built design and has 79 levers. The line to the left is from Stourbridge Junction and the line to the right is to Bromsgrove. The 6V70 has come from Bescot via Wedensbury and Brierly Hill, a line now closed, but potentially an important freight link between the north and south.

RIGHT: *Ledbury*: According to present plans, the signal box at Ledbury will be the last to be absorbed into the Cardiff (Wales) ROC in 2048. Built in 1885, it contains a 42-lever frame, and fringes with the 1984 OCS panel located in Hereford box to the west and Malvern Wells manual box to the east. Here, in 1985, a Hereford to Worcester stopping service leaves Ledbury station.

CAUTION TWO-WAY WORKING ON BOTH LINES

YEAR	BOXES TO BE TRANSFERRED
2012	Blakedown, Hartlebury, Kidderminster Junction, Kingswinford, Stourbridge Jn, Madeley Jn
2013	Bescot Down Tower, Bloxwich, Brereton Sidings, Hedensford, Walsall PSB
2015	Gloucester PSB, Saltley PSB, Wolverhapton PSB
2016	Claydon LNE Jn, Saltley PSB (second part), Alrewas, Fine Lane, Rodige, Banbury North & South, Leamington Spa PSB
2017	Birmingham New Street PSB, Aston SCC, Litchfield Trent Valley, Should merger into the Rugby ROC take place in 2018 then the boxes below would be added to the Rugby ROC. Rugby ROC
2015	Stafford No. 4, Stafford No. 5, Macclesfield
2017	Stoke SC
2019	Rugby SCC
2020	Basford Hall Jn, Crewe Coal Yard, Crewe Sorting Sidings North, Crewe Signalling Centre (Gresty Lane), Salop Goods Jn, Wembley Mainline SCC, Wembley Yard, Wembley Carriage Sheds North, Wembley Carriage Sheds South
2021	Crewe Signalling Centre (Crewe-Alsager), Winsford Jn, Oddingley
2022	Marston Vale SCC
2025	Marylebone IECC
2047	Kingsbury Shunt Frame & Tyseley No. 1, Norton Jn
2048	Droitwich Spa, Henwick, Malvern Wells, Newland East, Worcester Shrub Hill, Worcester, Tunnel Jn

Oddingley: Oddingley Crossing Box survives to this day and is not due to close until 2021. It is unusual in that there is no lever frame in the box. The crossing gates that it guards are kept closed to road traffic as their default position. Inside the box are Annett's Key Lock instruments, dating from 1969. If the crossing keeper wishes to open the gates to allow road vehicles across the main line, he or she may release the key if no train is approaching. Release of the key turns the protecting signals to red and they remain so until the gates are closed and the key replaced. In 1985, Class 25 No. 25191 passes with 7E45, the evening Speedlink from Severn Beach to Dringhouses.

FEATURED LINES
NORTON JUNCTION TO HEREFORD AND DROITWICH

The pocket of manual signalling around Worcester looks like it may be one of the last to survive in the UK if current Network Rail plans remain in place. While Ledbury in the west is to migrate to the Cardiff ROC in 2048, the signals in Worcester will be transferred to the Rugby ROC, also in 2048. In view of the fact that as plans stand this will be the last outpost of Victorian signalling in the UK, the area deserves a review. Having worked in Worcester in 1985, this selection of images covers the boxes in the area likely to become listed given their potential longevity.

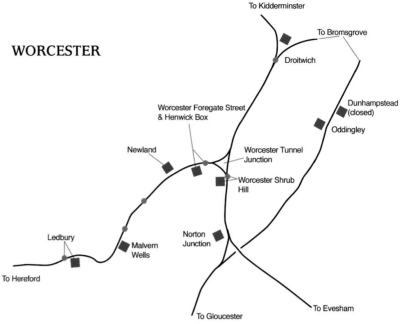

WORCESTER

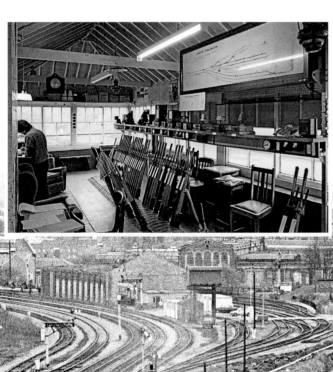

LEFT & BELOW: *Worcester*. Looking south from the tunnel mouth at Worcester, Class 25 No. 25060 accelerates away with the afternoon Worcester to Birmingham Curzon Street parcels. Worcester Tunnel Box, controlling the junction for Foregate Street and the locomotive depot, was built in 1905 and contains 58 levers. A long-forgotten visit in 1985 reveals gas lamps and fluorescent bulbs co-existing. Lever 58 is nearest the camera in this view of the frame and block shelf.

ABOVE: *Worcester*. The largest signal box in the area is Worcester Shrub Hill. It is difficult to photograph as it is tucked well back from the track south of Shrub Hill station. Built in 1935 to a Great Western brick design, it contains 84 levers. In this busy scene taken in 1985, HST Nos. 43133 and 43018 are just arriving with a Paddington to Worcester express, passing Class 37 No. 37166, which has just arrived with a parcels service from Birmingham Curzon Street depot. Another unidentified Class 37 is stabled behind the box awaiting a ballast working from Worcester yard.

BELOW: *Norton Junction*: Norton Junction signal box controls the junction of the Oxford line with the spur from the Bristol to Birmingham main line. It was built in 1908 and currently has a 19-lever frame, which is all that remains of a larger 33-lever installation. The single line to the left is from Evesham, while Class 56 No. 56068 is curving round from the Gloucester direction with 6M14, the daily Severn Tunnel Junction to Bescot Speedlink service, which will head on past Worcester and Droitwich, before heading for Stourbridge Junction and then Bescot.

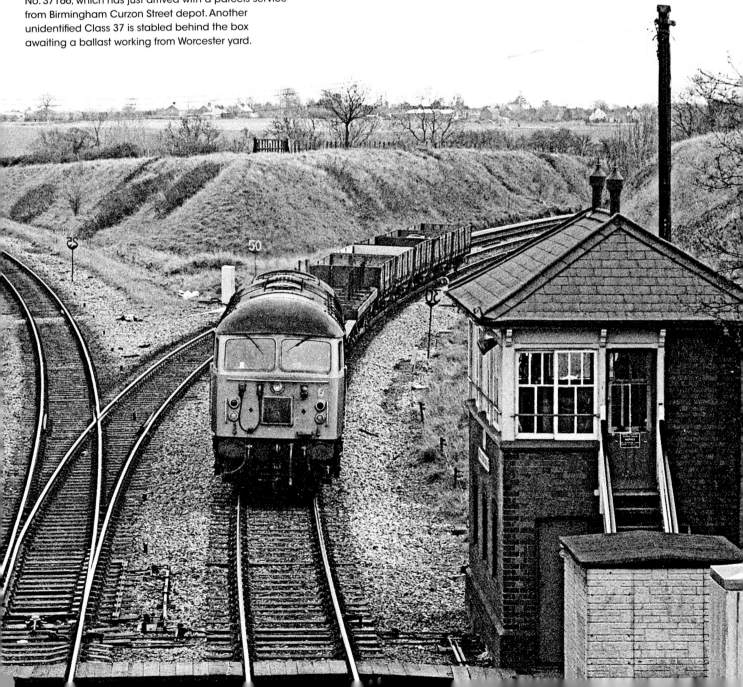

North West

ABOVE: *Chester:* Fifteen years on from the picture below left, in the summer of 1978, Class 40 No. 40126 comes off the Mickle Trafford line with a train of rock salt from Northwich. Trackwork and signalling remain largely unchanged since the steam era.

Morgan Sindall has constructed the three-storey steel-framed building which will eventually be home to 400 Network Rail employees with security very much in mind. Designed to be blast proof, with 24-hour security and multiple power supplies, there is even the facility to transfer control to another ROC via IP links in the event of a major catastrophe.

Siemens has provided the first workstation and interlockings at the ROC and an offline workstation adjacent to the main open plan signalling centre which allows training and problem-solving for new staff. Towards the end of 2014, Trans-Pennine and Northern Trains controllers moved into the ROC and by 2016 traction electrical control will be based within the ROC.

HISTORICAL SCHEMES
CHESTER

The resignalling of Chester was typical of many schemes in the 1970s and 1980s, driven by the desire to rationalise complex track and signalling infrastructure inherited from the steam era.

As such, the motivating force behind the scheme was infrastructure simplification and savings on staff and equipment, known today as 'OpEx' savings.

ABOVE: *Chester.* In a striking image from the early 1960s, BR standard No. 75012 accelerates out of Chester in the Helsby direction. Chester No.2 box and the serried ranks of semaphores remained largely unchanged at this location until 1984.
Photo: Vernon Murphy, M Rhodes & Steve Le Cheminant collection.

MANCHESTER ROC

During the summer of 2014, the new Manchester ROC opened on a brownfield site at Ashburys, on the old Manchester to Sheffield main line. The first signalling workstation was commissioned in July 2014 and controlled the line between Huyton and Roby on the original Liverpool and Manchester Railway route.

Eventually the ROC will be responsible for all traffic between Crewe in the south, Carlisle in the north, Todmorden to the east and the Welsh border in the west. For now the new Siemens Controlguide WestCad workstation is part of a broader capacity improvement on the Chat Moss line with the reintroduction of four running lines.

YEAR	BOXES TRANSFERRED
2013	Atherton Goods Yard, Blackrod Junction, Crow Nest Junction, Walkden to Preston PSB–Bare Lane, Hest Bank, Huncoat, Brierfield LCF to Chester PSB–Hootonto Castleton–Smithy Bridge
2014	Manchester East–Romiley to Burscough Bridge–Four Lane Ends XGB Brierfield to Preston PSB Huyton
2015	Manchester North PSB (Victoria–Miles Platting), Romily, St Helens station
2016	Ashton Moss North Junction, Denton Junction, Dinting station, Edge Hill, Liverpool Lime Street
2017	Allerton Junction, Bamber Bridge LCF, Blackpool North No. 2, Carleton Crossing, Salwick, Daisyfield Station, Ditton, Halton Junction, Horrocksford Junction, Kirkham North Junction, Manchester Piccadilly (Longsight-Picc), Poulton, Towneley XGB, Diggle Junction, Macclesfield, Runcorn, Speke Junction
2018	Burnside Higher XGB, Chinley, Earles Siding, Edale, Rainford Junction, New Mills Central, New Mills South Junction
2019	Astley, Baguley Fold, Bromley Cross LC, Eccles, Castleton East Junction, Manchester Piccadilly, Deansgate Junction, Greenbank, Mobberley, Northenden Junction, Plumley West, Edge Hill, Huyton, St Helens Station, Castleton East Junction, Vitirol Works, Rochdale
2020	Appleby North, Blea Moor, Bootle, Bransty, Culgaith, Drigg, Garsdale, Hellifield, Howe & Co's siding, Kirkby Stephen, Kirkby Thore, Low House Crossing, Maryport, Salcoats LC, Sellafield, Settle Junction, St Bees, Wigton, Workington Main No. 2, Workington Main No. 3
2021	Arnside, Askam, Barrow-in-Furness, Burscough Bridge, Carnforth station, Chapel Lane LC, Dalton Junction, Foxfield, Grange-over-Sands, Kirksanton XGB, Limestone Hall XGB, Millom, Parbold, Park South Junction, Silecroft, Skelly Crag XGB, Ulverston, Rainford Junction, Wigan Wallgate
2022	Grindleford
2024	Chester PSB, Ellesmere Port, Frodsham Junction, Helsby Junction, Norton (NW), Manchester East
2025	Edgeley Junction No.1, Edgeley Junction No. 2, Heaton Norris Junction, Carlisle PSB, Carlisle-Tebay, Carnforth Station Junction, Dee Marsh Junction, Buxton, Chapel-le-Frith, Furness Vale, Glazebrook East Junction, Great Rocks Junction, Mickle Trafford, Peak Forest South, Hazel Grove, Hunt's Cross, Norbury Hollow, Manchester South SC, Stockport No.1, Stockport No.2, Warrington Central
2026	Arpley Junction, Fiddlers Ferry, Midge Hall, Monks Siding, Preston PSB, Rufford (NW), Warrington PSB (Acton Grange)
2027	Bamber Bridge, Horrocksford Junction, Townley MCB
2030	Littons Mill Crossing, Warrington PSB (St Helens and Wigan NW)
2033	Merseyrail IECC, Hunt's Cross, Historical schemes

Chester Power signal box opened on May 6, 1984, and housed a Westinghouse NX panel controlling the station area as well as Mold Junction and Sandycroft.

Before the panel opened there had been minor changes in the area with Mold Junction No.4 box closing in 1978 and Chester No.3 box being amalgamated into Chester No.2 in December 1980. But in 1984 there were still five large signal boxes controlling Chester station: Chester No.2, 3A, 4, 5 and 6.

The largest of the boxes were No.2 with 180 levers and No.4 with 176, both double-manned. No.6 was also a large box which straddled the western approaches to Chester station and had 80 levers. The construction of a compact NX panel which could be single- or double-manned cut manpower costs for the Chester area to a fifth of their previous levels, justifying the investment.

BOLTON

In December 1985, the Bolton NX panel was commissioned heralding the end for three manual boxes, at Burnden Junction, Bolton West and Bolton East. This small panel, located in a portable building, lasted five years before functions were transferred to Manchester Piccadilly. The Bolton boxes are illustrated on page 59.

Chester. The 176 lever Chester No.4 box was a classical LNWR type 4 design, similar to large boxes at Llandudno Junction No. 2 (opened in 1898 with 118 levers expanded to 154 levers in 1921 and then reduced to 109 in 1968 and closed in 1985), Rhyl No. 2 (closed in 1990, but with 126 levers), Nuneaton No. 3 with 180 levers and closed in 1963, and Preston No. 1 with 162 levers and closed in 1973. This design of box included many of the largest manual lever signal boxes on the UK railway network; indeed, the world's largest surviving lever box at Shrewsbury Severn Bridge Junction, with 180 levers, is of the same basic design, albeit with a taller brick base.

ABOVE: *Chester.* Looking from waste ground between No. 6 and No. 4 signal box, the busy western approaches to Chester station are well seen. To the left is the locomotive depot, which was largely used for diesel multiple units by 1978, whlle beyond No. 4 box the platforms of Chester station can be made out.

RIGHT: *Chester.* This view taken from the Mickle Trafford line looking down on Chester motive power depot also shows Chester No.5 signal box. This was built to a non-standard design in 1874 as it was jointly owned by the LNW and the GW. It was apparently expanded in 1908 and 1915, and certainly the brickwork of the base seemed to show different ages and colours of bricks.

LEFT: *Chester.* Class 47 No. 47551 curves into Chester with a summer Saturday Holyhead to Manchester service in 1978. The No. 6 signal box was unusual in that it's 80-lever frame was suspended above the tracks on a steel frame.

Bolton: The S&T are at work and therefore the watchman has to wave for the approaching express at Burnden Junction, south of Bolton. The 80-lever box here was of Lancashire and Yorkshire railway design, dating back to 1905. It controlled the magnificent gantry under which Class 47 No. 47491 is about to pass with a Manchester to Edinburgh and Glasgow express. In 1983, the train split at Carstairs.

ABOVE: Bolton: The largest box in Bolton was Bolton East Junction. Built in 1902 this had a 145-lever frame. The frame was reduced to 88 levers in 1979 and then closed in 1985 when the Bolton NX panel was opened in a portable building. This then closed when control of Bolton was transferred to Manchester Piccadilly power box in 1990. Here, in November 1983, Class 40 No. 40096 is taxing the signalman as it shunts the 4J17 Barrow-in-Furness to Manchester Redbank sidings parcels train, which stopped at Bolton to pick up parcels stock from both the Up and Down sidings.

Bolton: One final view of the Bolton signals, taken in January 1985, shows the main gantry controlled by Bolton East Junction, under which Class 31 No. 31190 is passing with the Harwich to Glasgow boat train (a short-lived service). Behind the train is Burnden Junction and its gantry. Goodness knows how the passengers survived in electrically heated coaching stock when the Class 31 had no ETH equipment.

RIGHT: Bolton: Bolton West was a Westinghouse A, electro-pneumatic frame, built in 1903. The base of the box was rebuilt in brick in the 1930s to make it bombproof. The 83-lever frame controlled the junction of the Preston and Blackburn lines, and a Swindon DMU is seen here in March 1984 with a Blackpool to Manchester Victoria service passing the box.

ABOVE: *Buxton*: Buxton signal box used to control not only the passenger terminus but also access to the now-closed locomotive depot and a 12 track freight yard. The yard has been reduced to run-round loops for trains accessing the Hindlow branch and as a result the 1894 LNWR signal box has a reduced frame of 45 levers. However, below the floor the interlocking is still present for the original 60 lever frame.

RIGHT: Signaller Richard Stockton operates the single-line block token machine as a track inspection special leaves for the Peak Forest branch. The machine here is the 'partner' of the block token machine in Great Rocks, controlling the line through Topley Pike. Once Richard has removed his token, the line is occupied by whichever train carries it. Not until the token is replaced in the block token instrument, either at Buxton or in Great Rocks, can another be withdrawn to allow a train on to this single line section.

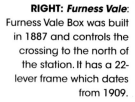

LEFT: *Chapel-en-le-Frith*: The signal box here is a 1957 BR (LMR) design with 20 levers. The box had to be rebuilt in 1957 after the famous railway accident, where a freight ran away down the 1-in-58 hill from Dove Holes summit towards Chapel-en-le-Frith. The driver, John Axon, heroically stayed with his runaway train trying to shut the regulator and avert disaster. He died in the attempt and was posthumously awarded the George Cross; a plaque commemorating his bravery is to be found here.

FEATURED LINE
PEAK FOREST AREA

Both the iconic Settle and Carlisle line and the intensely signalled Cumbrian Coast route will be controlled by the Manchester ROC, but the area of manual signalling that looks set to be the longest survivor in this area is around Buxton and Peak Forest.

The signal boxes here look set to keep working until 2025 according to present plans. Controlling several routes, we shall concentrate on the boxes under the care of the Peak Forest Local Area Manager or LOM, as well as a couple under neighbouring patches like Chinley which is managed by the Hope Valley LOM. Controlling a mixture of the busy Hope Valley route, the freight-only lines around Peak Forest and the rural terminus at Buxton, they make a fascinating collection and are illustrated on

RIGHT: *Furness Vale*: Furness Vale Box was built in 1887 and controls the crossing to the north of the station. It has a 22-lever frame which dates from 1909.

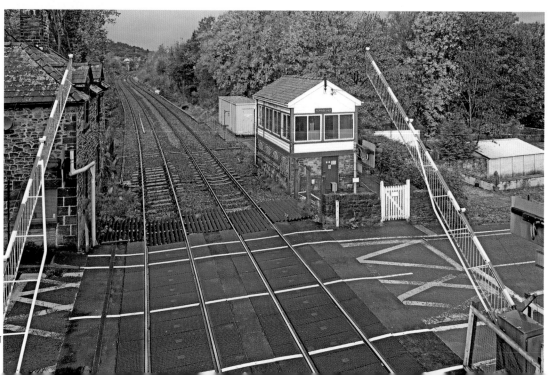

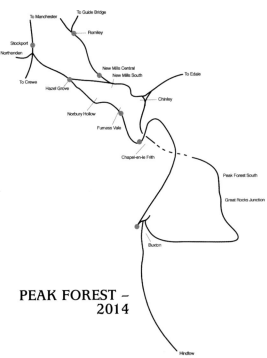

PEAK FOREST –
2014

ABOVE: *Chinley*: The signaller at Chinley has a quiet moment of contemplation in front of his 1982-installed OCS panel. The signal box was built in 1980 when the four-track Midland Railway main line at Chinley was rationalised. Chinley was the site of a fatal accident in 1986 when the 18.33 Sheffield to Manchester hit a light locomotive crossing from Chinley South to Chinley East. Unfortunately, the signalman on duty had a points failure and enthusiastically drove out to the junction and manually 'pumped' the points across to allow the light locomotive across Chinley East Junction. He did not however clip them in place and it seems that when he restored them to power, the road was set by the panel for the main line passenger train. The end result was one death and 25 injuries, four serious. As a result, training on OCS panels was improved and 'flank protection' introduced on junctions like Chinley East.

Great Rocks: Great Rocks Box was built in 1923, but had a flat roof fitted in the 1960s, replacing the more traditional Midland Railway gabled roof. The 34-lever frame controls access to Tunstead works and the branch to Buxton. In May 2013, Class 60 No. 60065 passes with 6F05, the Tunstead to Oakleigh limestone service.

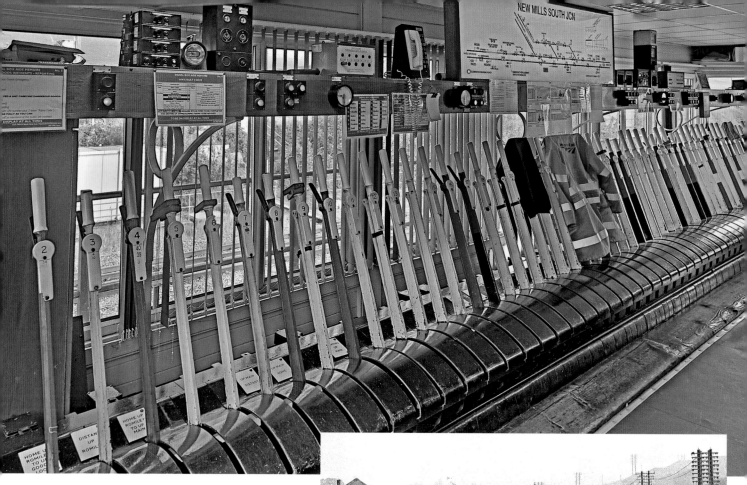

ABOVE AND RIGHT: *New Mills South*: The 1903 New Mills South Junction signal box along the Hope Valley line is the junction for the lines to Hazel Grove and direct to Manchester via New Mills Central. The 55-lever frame is one of the best kept on the line as this interior view from 2013 shows. Sadly, the traditional wooden windows have been replaced by modern plastic frames – excellent at keeping out draughts, but aesthetically not as pleasing. Back in July 1983, however, the box still had all its original features. On an unusually foggy day for July, Trans-Pennine DMU Nos. 51955, 59821, 59841 & 52098 pass with a Manchester to Sheffield and Cleethorpes service.

LEFT: *New Mills Central*: The 1924 vintage Midland Railway box at New Mills Central has 30 levers. Seen here in 2013, the passenger service to Manchester Piccadilly stands in the platform awaiting its return to the city.

ABOVE & LEFT: *Norbury Hollow*: Norbury Hollow Crossing is a rarely visited location. Here, a manual gated crossing is controlled by a six-levered cabin built to a BR (LMR) design in 1974. The highlight of any visit is a tour of the shrine erected in honour of signaller Ern Sweetmore's beloved Manchester United, followed by inspection of the sunflowers grown next to the box. To top it off, Ern makes an excellent cup of tea.

ABOVE: *Peak Forest*: Peak Forest South Junction is a 1925 Midland box with a 50-lever frame. Here, signaller Gary Steer makes us a cup of tea while local operations manager Anthony McIntyre records his visit in the TRB as well as recording my presence in the visitors' book. Peak Forest South is at the heart of the freight action generated by the local quarries.

RIGHT: A busy scene in June 2014 shows the signal box in the middle of the freight sidings. Class 66 No. 66139 has stood on the middle road for nearly an hour with 6H12, the Briggs sidings to Ashburys stone train. To its left is Class 66 No. 66221 with 6E08, a Ripple Lane to Peak Forest empty stone train, while Class 60 No. 60100 is being refuelled, having arrived with the 6F60 Lostock to Tunstead, and not due to leave until later in the evening with 6L27 the Peak Forest to Stourton stone service.

LEFT: *Romiley*: Dilip Tailor was on duty at Romiley Junction when we visited in 2013. The 1899 Midland-design signal box is hardly recognisable as such from the outside. The lever frame is long gone, having been replaced by an OCS panel in 1980. One aspect of railway signalling and the railway in general is the family histories of the workforce. Sometimes signalmen and women have worked in boxes over several generations. Dilip worked with Anthony MacIntyre's father when he was a signal man and now Anthony is visiting Romiley box as a local area manager. With concentration of signalling into 12 ROCs, such connections with the past are likely to be lost.

Scotland

GLASGOW ROC

The control of the railways in Scotland will be shared between two ROCs, one in Edinburgh and the other in Glasgow. The Glasgow ROC will be based around the West of Scotland Signalling Centre situated in the middle of the Cowlairs/Springburn triangle. The building and its facilities will need extension and upgrading, but will form the basis of the Glasgow ROC. It opened in 2008, taking control of Glasgow Central and the lines to Polmadie, Rutherglen, Shields & Paisley. In 2011 the lines to Gourock, Paisley & Wemyss Bay were added.

EDINBURGH ROC

The Edinburgh ROC will be based at the existing Edinburgh Signalling Centre, originally built to the south of Edinburgh Waverley in 1976. The NX panel installed at that time has been replaced by a new IECC signalling control system, initially covering Waverley itself and Midcalder in 2006. It was then extended to cover the line to Portobello in April 2007 and on to Granthouse in November 2007. In two stages in 2008 all the lines in Fife were added, followed by the route to Linlithgow in October 2008. Most recently, in 2013, the route from Glasgow Queen Street to Springburn and Gartshore have been added with a new workstation called the Cowlairs VDU. Ironic given that it controls the trains passing in front of the Glasgow ROC.

LEFT: *Inverness*: A portrait of a loco box, with Class 26 No. 26013 awaiting entry into the shed at Inverness in 1979.

BELOW LEFT: The Highland Railway signal box at the southern entrance to Inverness station dates back to the 19th century and had a 64-lever frame from 1904. As well as controlling departures from Inverness to Perth and Aberdeen, it (as its name suggests) controlled access to the locomotive depot and works. In September 1979, Class 47 No. 47550 awaits departure with the Clansman to London Euston, while the station pilot Class 08 No. 08728 shunts coaching stock past Class 26 No. 26014, which is stabled in the station.

HISTORICAL SCHEMES
INVERNESS AND ABERDEEN

In July and August 1981, the wonderful gantries controlling Aberdeen station were removed as a new NX panel was opened to control the Aberdeen area. The boxes at Aberdeen Centre, North and South closed as did Ferryhill Junction and Craiginches North & South. Resignalling further west in the Inverness area started in October 1984 with the introduction of RETB between Dingwall and Kyle of Lochalsh and Dingwall and Garve. In the summer of 1985 this was extended to Wick and Thurso. Then in February 1987, the Inverness NX panel was opened, initially replacing Welsh's Bridge signal box on February 15, that year. A few weeks later on March 8, the boxes at Culloden Moor, Milburn Junction and Loco (Inverness) closed, followed by Inverness Rose Street on March 22. This development left the line between Inverness and Aberdeen as the most northerly route controlled by manual signals.

RIGHT: *Welsh's Bridge*: A second view of the Clansman on September 5, 1979 with Class 47 No. 47550 making some smoke as it passes Welsh's Bridge signal box. This 95-lever signal box dated back to 1898 and was the largest in the area. It was literally just a couple of hundred yards west of the loco box and 400 yards from Milburn Junction on the other side.

LEFT: *Welsh's Bridge & Milburn Junction:* The intensive nature of the signalling can be judged from this view, taken standing at the foot of loco box steps. Welsh's Bridge is seen to the left of the image, and beyond it the concrete structure of Milburn Junction box is visible. Milburn Junction was to a war design and opened in 1943; it contained 80 levers. In this view taken on the morning of September 13, 1979, Class 40 No. 40078 is moving a couple of Class 47 locomotives onto the depot, while Class 40 No. 40154 awaits departure with a Glasgow express. Class 26 No. 26014 is at the head of a train to Aberdeen. With departures to London, Edinburgh, Glasgow and Aberdeen in quick succession, the station throat was a busy place first thing in the morning.

LEFT: *Aberdeen*: Nestling under the road bridge to the north of Aberdeen station, was Aberdeen North signal box. It had a 150-lever frame and its size is an indication of how busy the railway north from Aberdeen used to be. By June 1981, when this image was taken, the line north to Kittybrewster and Dyce had been reduced to a single track and most of the levers in the box were 'white' or out of use. Class 26 No. 26033 arrives with an Inverness to Aberdeen passenger service.

LEFT: *Aberdeen*: Aberdeen South – the sturdy brick walls of Aberdeen South signal box can just be seen on the extreme right of this 1981 image of Class 47 No. 47420 arriving with the 05.50 King's Cross to Aberdeen. This train was a favourite among enthusiasts in 1981 as it was often hauled by a Deltic as far as York and on occasion the Deltic continued north to Edinburgh and even Aberdeen; sadly not on this day. The signal box was built to an LMS design, introduced during the Second World War and aimed to protect against bombing. The box had 150 levers, a reduction from the former 240-lever frame that had been in operation at this location.

ABOVE: *Ferryhill*: Aberdeen Ferryhill taken from the balcony of Ferryhill Junction signal box, looking north, on March 24, 1981, shows the unusual sight of two freight trains. Class 47 No. 47131 winds out onto the mainline with 4V37, the daily Aberdeen to Glasgow freightliner train. Its departure has led to Class 27 No. 27018 being held on the mainline with an empty ballast train from Insch to Craiginches yard.

LEFT: Aberdeen Ferryhill (interior) – the south end of the frame at Ferryhill Junction is seen in this 1981 view, just months before the box closed. It had controlled the junction of the line to Ballater, closed in 1966, but for the remaining 15 years of its working life just controlled access to Ferryhill locomotive depot.

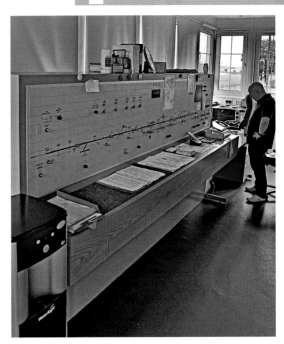

RIGHT: *Dyce*: In 2007, the manual frame at Dyce was removed and replaced by a new NX panel. The extensive single line, shown clearly on the panel, is a problem for the ambition to reintroduce an hourly service between Inverness and Aberdeen, but even more so for the burgeoning commuter traffic from Inverurie.

BELOW LEFT & BOTTOM LEFT: *Elgin*: Elgin Centre box and ground frame – the 50-lever frame of Elgin Centre signal box is all that is holding the wooden structure up now. Amazingly, this box closed in 1973, but still stands to the east of Elgin station surrounded by trees and shrubs. Opposite is the old Elgin East station, closed to passengers in 1968, but used for many years after that as a goods office. The goods yard east of Elgin station was mothballed for many years after grain and whisky traffic ended in the early 1990s, but has recently been refurbished by DB Schenker for occasional military traffic. As with many sparsely used facilities, access is now controlled by a ground frame, usually operated by the train crew or a mobile shunter, who drives to the location whenever a freight is expected. The ground frame at Elgin East has just four levers.

ABOVE: *Dyce*: A sense of the former importance of Dyce Junction is seen by the size of the signal box. It had controlled the junction with the branch lines to Peterhead and Fraserburgh, but by the time this view was taken in 1988 the frame in the signal box had been reduced to just 26 levers. Class 47 No. 47644 arrives with an Aberdeen to Inverness service which ran two hourly at this time.

RIGHT: *Huntly*: The signal box here dates back to 1890, but was only a level crossing gate box until 1970, when it was upgraded to become the only signal box in Huntly. At this stage a 25-lever frame was installed to control both the mainline and access to the extensive goods yard here. This 2014 view shows an Aberdeen to Inverness passenger service passing the box. The lighting and earthworks of the long-disused goods yard are seen on the left.

FEATURED LINES
INVERNESS TO ABERDEEN

As mentioned above, the line between Inverness and Aberdeen, is the most northerly route in the country to remain manually signalled and Elgin at its centre is Britain's most northerly surviving manual signal box. The line between Scotland's two northern centres fell into decline in the 1970s and 80s and much of it was singled. The service dropped to two hourly and was slow. Such has been the resurgence of rail passenger traffic however, that in 2013 the line attracted £170 million investment. This will be used to re-double the track between Aberdeen and Inverurie. There will be signalling improvements at Elgin and the relocation of Forres station which will remove a tight curve and consequent speed restriction.

There are plans for new stations at Kintore and Dalcross and extension of platforms at Elgin and Insch. The whole five-year package is aimed at providing an hourly service between Inverness and Aberdeen and cutting the journey time to two hours. Part of the improvements are likely to see closure of the signal boxes at Nairn and Forres with control moved to Inverness in 2016. At the eastern end of the line the boxes at Inverurie and Dyce are likely to close too with control transferred to Aberdeen panel. It is however envisaged that the remaining manual boxes will survive for another decade until 2024 or 2025.

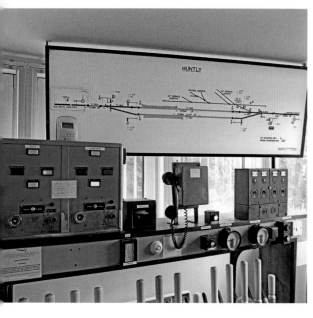

ABOVE: *Huntly*: Scottish Region Tokenless Block – the Inverness to Aberdeen line has many single line sections and these are controlled in two ways. That between Nairn and Forres uses the traditional single line token. In this system the signaller releases a token from the block instrument in the signal box and hands it to the driver, giving authority to be on the single line section. Not until the token is relinquished at the other end of the single line, and replaced into the matching block token instrument, can another train be given another token and thereby access to the line.

TOP RIGHT: *Huntly*: One exception to this rule was demonstrated to me by Kenneth Gray, the signalman at Huntly for the last 25 years. Sometimes, access to the single line section at Huntly might be needed for shunting movements at the goods yard. To allow access onto the single line for the first few hundred yards, even if a train to Kennethmont was still on the single line section, heading east, there is an Annett's 'shunting key'. This allows access onto the single line once it is fitted into the signal lever removed from the signal and given to the driver. It signifies that the section of single line is clear or occupied by a train proceeding away from the station. Once it is released from the frame, it locks the section signal and prevents acceptance of another train.

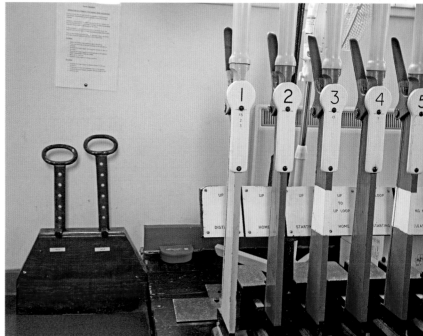

ABOVE MIDDLE: *Huntly*: A second system used on the line (and also the Highland mainline between Perth and Inverness) is the Scottish tokenless block. The blue boxes on the right of this interior view control this. Instead of an actual token, the 'token' which allows a train onto the single line is given electronically by depressing the plunger on these blue boxes. Once the plunger has been activated, no other train can gain access to the single line until the signaller at the other end of the section confirms the train has left the single track and then depressed the matching plunger on his tokenless block instrument.

ABOVE RIGHT: *Huntly*: Signal wire adjusters: The wires which control manual signals change in length with fluctuations in temperature. As it gets colder they shorten and conversely as it warms up they lengthen. The most common way of adjusting the tension in the signal wire is with a wheel or a wrench which locks into rods in the box floor. In Huntly (and several other Scottish boxes), a simple lever system is employed as seen here at the western end of the signal frame.

ABOVE & RIGHT: *Insch*: The signal box at Insch dates back to 1886, but was extensively refurbished in 2000. It contains a 20-lever frame, installed in 1969. The double-track mainline from Kennethmont is reduced to a single line as far as Inverurie and this is controlled by the Scottish tokenless block system.

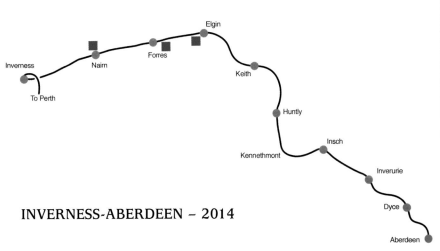

INVERNESS-ABERDEEN – 2014

ABOVE: *Keith*: Inside the box at Keith Junction is a 40-lever frame, installed in 1969. In 1969 and 1970, as a result of the Beeching closures along the Inverness to Aberdeen route, and in an attempt to reduce costs, signal boxes were reduced in size or signalling was concentrated on one cabin, where once there had been two or three.

LEFT: *Nairn*: The centralising of the signalbox to Nairn station has brought the unusual juxtaposition of a state-of-the-art Westcad VDU screen to control trains and a traditional block token instrument. Not just that, but to the left of the VDU screen the old signal register and booking box are still in use. Lifting the lid of the booking box, inscriptions from signallers dating back half a century can be found. One rest day, relief signaller C M Innes inscribed each year he completed from 1969 to 1994, while the signaller on duty in 2014, George Mannes, could identify at least one close relative who had inscribed the lid in the past.

ABOVE: *Kennethmont*: The signal box here dates from 1888 and as mentioned elsewhere was the recipient of a reduced-size frame of 20 levers as part of the 1969 rationalisation along the route. It was refurbished along with many boxes along the line in 2000 when uPVC windows were fitted and toilet and kitchen facilities upgraded.

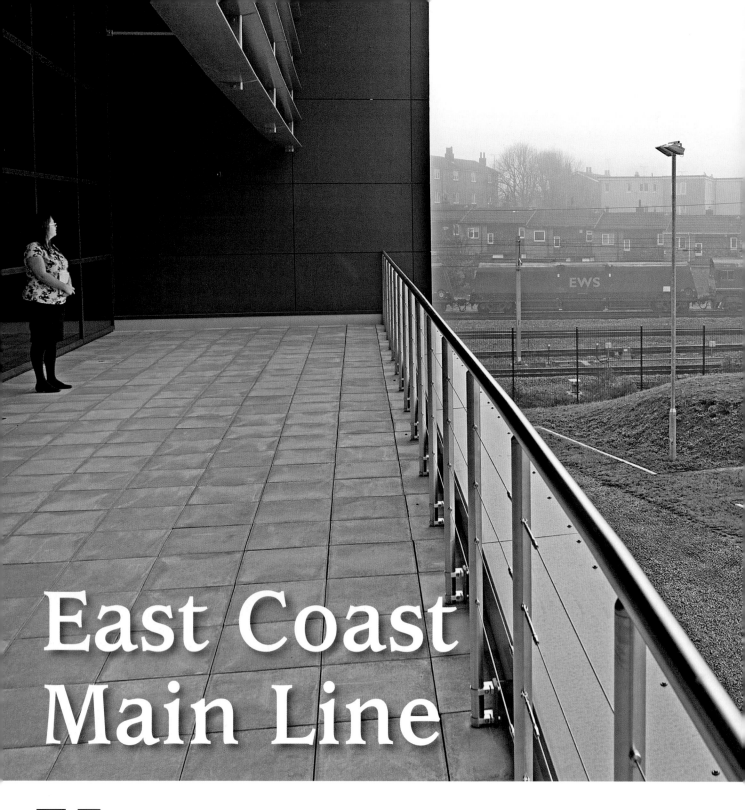

East Coast Main Line

York has long been a place of signalling superlatives. The largest ever traditional lever signal box was located south of the station on almost the same site as the current ROC. Called Locomotive Yard Signal Box, it contained 295 levers and controlled the southern approaches to York station as well as access to York South shed.

The box was replaced in April 1951 by the world's largest interlocking. The OCS panel (one control switch) signalled from Skelton Junction in the north to Chaloners Whin Junction in the south, a total of 33 track miles. At three times the size of London Liverpool Street panel, the new panel replaced eight mechanical signal boxes with a total of 868 levers. Decommissioned in May 1989 and replaced by the York IECC, this panel is now history, but the area will soon be controlled by the largest ROC in the UK, another signalling record for York.

The York ROC opened in January 2015 and is a remarkable building, costing £38 million and built by BAM construction. I was privileged to visit the facility in November 2014, while it was still being fitted out. It is difficult to imagine such a building, part of the York Campus which also includes a state of the art training centre, as a signal box. It is much more akin to the European Laparoscopic Surgery Training Centre located in Hamburg than any signal box I have ever visited!

The step change from Victorian railway to the 21st century is stark. The commitment of Network Rail to utilise the most modern technology and control systems for Britain's overcrowded railways is impressive. The arrival area at the ROC is spacious and decorated in a stylish, yet minimalist way. The reception desk is staffed by two ladies who would not look out of place in a big London office like NICE or the MHRA. A visitor's badge is handed over and I am seated watching a 40-inch

ABOVE: Louise Gummerson looks out from the patio at York ROC as Class 66 No. 66137 passes with a Tees Dock to Drax coal train. Eventually this will provide an area for coffee and lunch with tables and chairs – hard to imagine on a dull November day.

YORK ROC
BOXES ABSORBED INTO THE ROC

YEAR	
2012	To York IECC – Horsforth, Rigton, Heck Ings GC, Cutsyke Junction
2014	Crofton Old Station GC, Joan Croft GC, Godnow Bridge, Medge Hall, Bonsall Lane, North Carr,
	To Doncaster PSB – Dormer Green, Balne, Moss, Balne Lowgate, Barcroft, Fenwick, Heyworth, Noblethorpe
	To Lincoln SCC – Bearty Fen, Blankney, Blotoft, Blue Gowts, Brewery Lane, Cheal Road, Church Lane, Flax Mill, Gainsborough Lea Road, Golden High Hedges, Gosberton, Littleworth, Mill Green, Park Road, Rowston, Saxilby, Scopwick, Sleaford North, Sleaford South, Spalding, St James Deeping, Stow Park, Sykes Lane, Water Drove
	To Ferrybridge SB – Hensal, Sudforth Lane, England Lane, Heck Lane, High Eggborough
	To Selby – Henwick Hall, Thorpe Gates, Barlby, Burn Lane, Sandhill Lane
	To Bowesfield – Urlay Nook
2015	Cutsyke LC
2016	Appleby Lincs, Barnetby East, Barton Road GC (close crossing), Beckingham, Beighton Station, Bonsall Lane GC, Brigg, Brocklesby Junction, Broomfleet, Cave GB, Crabley Creek, Elsham, Gainsborough, Gainsborough Trent Junction, Gilberdyke Junction, Green Oak Goit LC, Immingham East, Kirton Lime Sidings, Kiveton Park, Marsh Junction, Melton Lane, New Barnetby GC, Northorpe, Oxmardyke GB, Pasture Street, Roxton Sidings, Saltmarshe, Sheffield PSB, Stallingborough, Ulceby Junction, Welton GB, Woodburn Junction, Woodhouse, Wrawby Junction, York IECC
2017	Batley, Belasis Lane (signal box already closed), Billingham-on-Tees, Bowesfield, Crag Hall, Diggle Junction, Grangetown, Greatham, Halifax, Hebden Bridge, Huddersfield, Longbeck, Lowgates, Middlesborough, Mill Lane, Milner Royd, Norton-on-Tees East, Norton-on-Tees South, Norton-on-Tees Station, Norton-on-Tees West, Nunthorpe, Redcar, Ryhope Grange, Tees Yard, Whitehouse
2018	Barnsley East, Grindleford, Healey Mills, Horbury Junction, Totley Tunnel, Wakefield Kirkgate, Wooley Coal Sidings
2019	Belmont GB, Castleford, Cattal, Hammerton Road GC, Hammerton, Harrogate, Hessay GB, Knaresborough, Marston Moor GB, Poppleton, Starbeck, Whixley GB, Wilstrop GB, Ferrybridge, Prince of Wales, Ancaster, Rauceby, Sleaford East, Sleaford West, Eastfield, Peterborough PSB, Woodcroft
2020	Bardon Mill, Blaydon, Brampton Fell, Corby Gates, Denton Village, Haltwhistle, Haydon Bridge, Hexham, Lane Head, Low Row, Milton Village, Prudhoe, Wylam, Doncaster PSB, Norton GB, Bellwater Junction, Heckington, Hubberts Bridge, Sibsey, Skegness, Thorpe Culvert, Wainfleet, West Street Junction, Carlton GB, Claypole GB, Grassthorpe Lane GC, Helpston GB, Finningley GB, Ranskill GB
2021	Butterwell B shunt box, Spittal, Tweedmouth, Hull Paragon, Bedlington North, Bedlington South, Freemans, Hirst Lane, Marcheys House, Newsham, North Seaton, Winnin
2022	Gascoine Wood, Milford, Keadby Canal, Scunthorpe PSB, Holton le Moor, Langworth, Wickenby
2023	Great Coates No.1, Pyewipe Road
2025	Beverley, Bridlington, Driffield, Gristhorpe, Hessle Road, Hull River Bridge, Lebberston Road, Seamer, Barton Hill, Common Road, Howsham, Kirkham Abbey, Malton, Strensall, Weaverthorpe
2026	Thrumpton
2027	Ferryhill, Heaton Control Tower, Tyneside IECC, Heighington, Shildon
2029	Alnmouth
2044	Seaham
2051	Selby Swing Bridge
2056	Morpeth

television displaying BBC News 24 and offered a most acceptable cup of coffee.

The York ROC will employ upwards of 400 people when fully operational with a minimum of 87 on site at any one time.

It will eventually control the ECML from King's Cross to the Scottish border where it will fringe with the Edinburgh ROC. Along the route, all the lines in Lincolnshire and South Humberside will be controlled from York as will those in north Yorkshire and north Humberside. At its southern extent, the ROC will fringe with Three Bridges at King's Cross, while further north the Romford ROC will fringe to the east and the Derby ROC to the west. In South Yorkshire, the area formerly controlled by the Sheffield power signal box will move to York ROC and the fringe ROC here will be in Manchester, as indeed will be the fringe ROC on the Newcastle to Carlisle line.

HISTORICAL SCHEMES
BARROW HILL

Sheffield power signal box, which opened in January 1973, is due to transfer to the York ROC in 2016. Between 1979 and 1982 the panel took over control of the 'Old Road' between Rotherham and Chesterfield via Barrow Hill. In doing so 16 classic Midland signal boxes were closed and a dramatic patch of semaphore signalling at Barrow Hill abolished. In July 1979 the boxes around Rotherham at Masborough North and South, Masborough Station North, Masborough Station South Junction and Parkgate Junction were closed. This was followed in November 1981 by closure of the boxes at Barrow Hill Junction, Barrow Hill South, Dunston & Barlow North, Foxlow Junction, Hall Lane Junction, Reninshaw Park Goods Junction and Whittington. In August 1982 Markham colliery sidings box closed with control of the branch transferred to Seymour Junction box. Finally in October 1982 the boxes at Treeton North and South and Barrow Hill Up sidings closed. Seymour Junction signal box lasted until 2006 when it was opened for a railtour. Sadly it was damaged by fire shortly after its last working day and had to be demolished.

ABOVE & BELOW: *Foxlow Junction*: To the north of Barrow Hill on the main line to Rotherham, the next box was Foxlow Junction. This 1980 view shows the 50-lever frame (albeit with several levers missing). Meanwhile, outside Class 44 No. 44004 passes with 7Z12 and extra unfitted freight from Toton to Tinsley. The line to the left runs round to Hall Lane Junction and the branch to Seymour yard and Bolsover.

LEFT: *Barrow Hill Junction*: A Mountsorrel to Doncaster ballast service made up of 'Dogfish' vacuum-fitted wagons passes Barrow Hill Junction signal cabin in June 1980, hauled by Class 31 No. 31211. Opened in 1928, it was originally called Staveley Junction, but with closure of the iron works of the same name it became Barrow Hill Junction. It had a 100-lever frame, larger than most Midland Railway boxes. In the distance, above the last wagon of the train, is Barrow South signal box, while the corner of Barrow Hill Up Sidings box is just visible on the extreme left of the image. The semaphores at Barrow Hill are an iconic image of the Victorian era railway, which disappeared in 1981.

BELOW: *Hall Lane Junction*: Class 20 Nos. 20058 and 20026 pass Hall Lane Junction signal box on June 2, 1980, running engine and van from Barrow Hill to Seymour Junction, from where they will collect coal from the Bolsover branch. Two eminent photographers can be seen above the parapet, both with hair in those days – Paul Shannon and Kim Fullbrook opting for the going away shot. The small Midland Railway cabin is fringed with Barrow Hill Junction to the west and Foxlow Junction to the north. To the south was the brick-built Seymour Junction box, which had 95 levers and controlled the large yard of the same name.

HISTORICAL SCHEMES
LINCOLN

Lincoln was resignalled in 2008. The £55 million scheme saw the closure of the boxes at Pelham Street Junction, Lincoln High Street, East Holmes and West Holmes. The new Lincoln signalling centre was opened on September 1, 2008, after a six-week engineering possession of Lincoln and the surrounding area during which no trains ran. Since 2008, the Lincoln signalling centre has taken over control of much of the 'Joint' line from Doncaster to Peterborough via Sleaford. The new centre will itself be absorbed by the York ROC in the next decade.

LEFT: *Pelham Box Junction (Lincoln)*: The 1883-built Great Northern signal box closed on July 19, 2008. It was demolished on August 19, even before the new Lincoln signalling centre opened. It contained a 1918 vintage 100-lever frame seen here during a visit in the 1990s.

BELOW: *Pelham Box Junction (Lincoln)*: Class 56 No. 56116 passes the box on July 26, 1996, with 6D90, the thrice-weekly Immingham to Gainsborough oil train. Access to the oil depot at Gainsborough Lea Road could only be made from the south, necessitating the circuitous route via Lincoln.

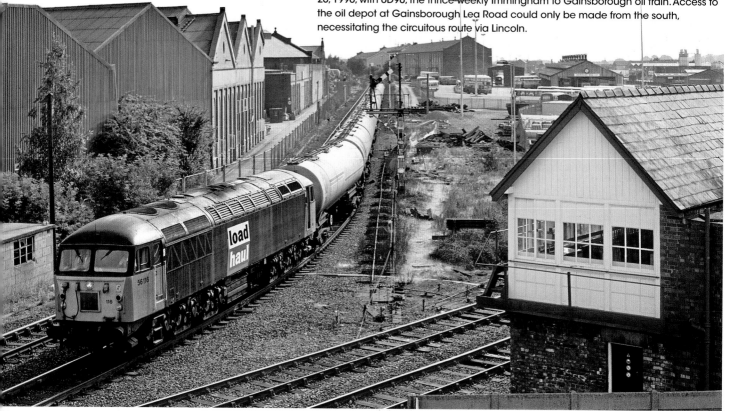

RIGHT & BELOW: *West Holmes (Lincoln)*: It is on waste ground near the site of the former West Holmes signal box that the new Lincoln signalling centre has been built. West Holmes itself was a 69-lever signal box, opened in 1882. It used to control the western access to Holmes Yard, long since lifted in the picture of Class 144 No.144005 with a Sheffield to Lincoln train, and now largely covered by the University of Lincoln.

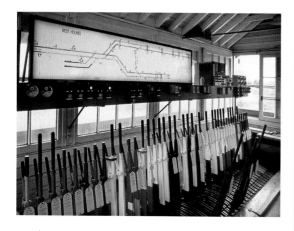

HIGH STREET

ABOVE: *High Street (Lincoln)*: Two for the price of one in this view taken in 1996. A Nottingham to Lincoln service crosses the high street and the eponymously named signal box. Opened in 1883, the box had 36 levers. Just a couple of hundred yards behind it, the traffic is already crossing the tracks at East Holmes.

BELOW: *East Holmes (Lincoln)*: Passing East Holmes in 1986 are Class 37 Nos. 37221 and 37202 at the head of 6H52, a West Burton to Peterborough fly ash service. The Great Northern box opened in 1873 and had 35 levers.

EAST HOLMES

FEATURED LINES
IMMINGHAM AND GRIMSBY

One of the most varied concentrations of manual signalling still in operation is on South Humberside. The centre of activity is Barnetby. Lines to the east are all manually signalled and indeed heading west from Wrawby Junction, Victorian boxes and manual signals can be found on the routes to Scunthrope, Gainsborough and Lincoln. This section gives a fleeting overview of the 18 boxes still in action east of Wrawby Junction. Many have only 12-18 months left and the area is well worth a visit.

ABOVE: *Barnetby East*: This 1917 Great Central signal box has 72 levers and, as can be seen from this image, leans to one side a bit. The longest pull is signal 19 which has a wire that runs halfway to Wrawby Junction and back. The hardest signal to pull is, however, No.21, the Up starter, while No.26, the Down main crossover, is the most difficult point to change. Class 60 No. 60074 passes with an Immingham Docks to Santon iron ore train on June 2, 2011.

LEFT: *Great Coates*: By 2013, when the interior view was taken, the line past Great Coates was normally closed. It may reopen to regular traffic if plans to make more use of the Immingham light railway for oil and steel traffic materialise. The 1909-built box still has its 23-lever frame and if freight to and from the Immingham area continues to increase it may yet get a second lease of life before closure.

BELOW: *Great Coates*: Sidings No.1: Back in 1990, the yard at Great Coates was still busy with steel traffic and also saw daily trains from Immingham with general goods. On March 6, 1990, the yard pilot is Class 08 No. 08.388. The 1910 cabin is still manned for two shifts daily.

ABOVE: *Brocklesby*: The 1915 Great Central signal box used to contain 95 levers. In 1998 these were, however, replaced by an NX panel seen in this interior view from 2013. The signaller has railways in the blood as her father was also a signalman.

BELOW: *Brocklesby*: The cabin at Brocklesby is seen from outside in this view taken in July 2006. Class 66 No. 66217 is curving off the Immingham Docks branch with an Immingham to Drax coal train.

ABOVE: *Barrow Road Crossing*: Signalman 'Robbie' releases the manual gates at Barrow Road Crossing in July 2012. The box once had a 28-lever frame when the docks were open, but this has now been reduced to just eight. The cabin itself was built in 1885 and is now only disturbed by the two-hourly service to Barton-upon-Humber.

LEFT & BELOW: *Goxhill*: The signal box here has 36 levers and was built by the GC in 1910. It is unusual in having crossing gates controlled by a wheel. The mechanism is much simpler than the cantilevered system at Stallingborough (see elsewhere in this section). These two images show signalman Graham winding the gates closed and then the gates opening again, just seconds after a Barton-upon-Humber to Cleethorpes train has passed. This method of gate operation is much more efficient than manual gates, where the signaller is required to leave the box and open and close the gates manually; and to some extent it is also more efficient than electronically operated gates, which almost always have significant delay before they open after a train has passed. This is in stark contrast to manually wound gates which keep the signaller warm and dry in the box, yet may be opened with the train less than 100 yards away (as illustrated) – Victorian mechanical engineering at it's best.

ABOVE: *Garden Street (Grimsby)*: The fourth and most easterly box in Grimsby was Garden Street. Built in 1880 by the MSLR, it had 39 levers. Resignalling from here to Cleethorpes came in 1985 when Pasture Street NX panel was opened, controlling all the lines from Garden Street to Cleethorpes. Then in September 1993, the four boxes in the Grimsby station area at Lillifield, Friargate, Wellowgate and Garden Street were closed, and control transferred to Pasture Street panel.

RIGHT: *Wrawby Junction*: A box with a view – back in 2008, Class 60 No. 60100 approaches Wrawby Junction with an Immingham to Santon iron ore train.

ABOVE: *Friargate & Lillifield Lane (Grimsby)*: Grimsby boasted four signal boxes within half a mile of one another. Looking west in 1990, this view of Class 150 No. 150102 with a Sheffield to Cleethorpes train shows Friargate Crossing and just a couple of hundred yards away Lillifield Lane Crossing. Friargate box was built by the Manchester Sheffield and Lincoln Railway (MSLR) in 1884 and had a 14-lever frame. Just 50 yards behind the photographer was Wellowgate crossing, controlling the western access to Grimsby station and also built by the MBLR and with 30 levers.

LEFT: *Immingham West*: Signaller King is checking on 'Trust', the Network Rail computer, to see what traffic is due when we visited in April 2013. Immingham West had an IFS panel fitted to replace its manual levers as long ago as 1971. The IFS panel seen here was installed in 2006 as a replacement to reflect the opening of the new Humber Bulk Handling Terminal and the associated sidings. There is, as yet, no clear date for the migration of Immingham West and nearby Reception Sidings signal box to the York ROC, because while they are both manned by Network Rail, they belong to ABP.

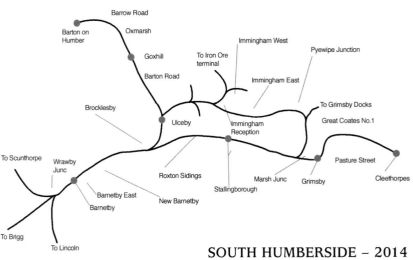

SOUTH HUMBERSIDE – 2014

LEFT AND BELOW: *Pyewipe Junction*: Mothballed for the last couple of years, Pyewipe Junction signal box controls the junction between the Grimsby Light Railway and the line to Grimsby Docks or West Marsh yard. Back in 1996, Class 60 No. 60038 passes the crossing under the watchful eye of the signalman with 6D85, the Tioxide sidings to Roxby landfill train. The mechanical winding gear for the crossing gates was temperamental at the time and the signaller had to manually push the gates home. Fast forward 16 years to 2013 and a visit to the box revealed the gate wheel made by the Railway Signal Company in Liverpool was in excellent order, with leather pouches poised to hand out single line tokens. The box was built in 1958 and has 20 levers in a frame of the same year.

BELOW: *Wrawby Junction*: Perhaps the best known view of Wrawby Junction is from Barnetby station. Here, in October 2012, the Rail Head Treatment Train or 'leaf buster' approaches Barnetby, hauled by DRS Class 20 Nos. 20302 and 20301. The train is working as 3S13 from Wrenthorpe to Grimsby and will be back in an hour or so, running in the other direction as 3S14 from Grimsby to York.

ABOVE: *New Barnetby*: Class 153 No. 153379 passes the manned crossing at New Barnetby. Like so many little-used level crossings around the country, this is manned 24 hours a day at enormous cost. Accommodation is often provided in these standard green portable buildings, with toilet, kitchen and living facilities for the signaller.

ABOVE: *Roxton Sidings*: Perhaps the most isolated signal box in this section, guarding as it does a rarely used road crossing. The sidings of the signal box name are long gone. It was built in 1883 by the Manchester, Sheffield and Lincoln Railway and has 18 levers and a manual gate wheel.

ABOVE AND BELOW: *Stallingborough*: The current Stallingborough signal box was built in 2007 to a Network Rail gabled design, aimed at mimicking the style of a Victorian box. It contains an NX panel and was needed quite simply because the old Stallingborough box was falling down. Back in 1996, the signalman joked with me that they raced marbles from one end of the box to the other, so steep was the slope! These two images show the 1884 MS&LR box with its cantilevered crossing gate wheel, similar to that at Pyewipe Junction. The old box had 20 levers and, as the exterior view shows, had a significant list away from the main line, even back in 1996.

ABOVE: *Immingham Reception Sidings*: Above the brick base, the signal box at Immingham Reception Sidings is kept in excellent condition and benefited from a repaint in 2006. This view shows Class 66 No. 66033 leaving with an old-style MGR to Eggborough. A Freightliner Class 66 is loading new high-capacity, 100-ton cal wagons on the left, while the EWS-liveried yard pilot is shunting steel wagons on the right.

LEFT: *Immingham Reception Sidings*: Veteran signalman Roy Kaminski keeps the coal trains moving on a sweltering evening in June 2012. With the mercury nudging 32 degrees in the early evening, he resorted to shorts, which he wished he hadn't worn when he realised he was about to be photographed. Immingham Reception Sidings is not only the last of the GC electro-pneumatic frames in operation, but also the 91-lever frame is complemented by two small panels (NX & IFS) to control the lines to Lindsey and Humber oil refineries.

ABOVE: *Ulceby*: During my most recent visit to Ulceby signal box there was a points failure – fortunately having the acting local area manager with me, he was able to get trackside within 10 minutes and remedy the failure to "keep the job going" as he put it. The signaller at Ulceby contemplates his box diagram that day as a DBS Class 66 stands at the signal with a Scunthorpe to Immingham empty coal train, waiting for the errant set of points to be fixed.

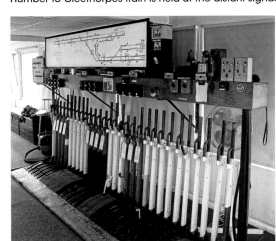

ABOVE: *Ulceby*: The view from the signal box steps shows the mix of manual and modern signals at Ulceby. Class 66 No. 66607 rounds the corner from Immingham with 6R14, an Immingham to Ferrybridge coal train. In the distance a Barton-upon-Humber to Cleethorpes train is held at the distant signal.

ABOVE: *Marsh Junction*: The signal box at Marsh Junction is perhaps one of the most inaccessible on the network, protected as it is by 10-foot high pallisade fencing. This may be a reflection of the local environment, but certainly to reach it is a bit like entering a high-security prison. Built in 1908 by the Great Central, its 44-lever frame is well seen here during a 2012 visit. A new road bridge to an industrial estate next to the old West Marsh railway yard may provide good views of the box and junction in the future.

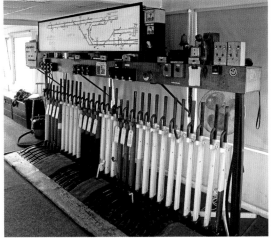

LEFT: *Ulceby*: The box at Ulceby Junction was built by the Great Central in 1910 and contains a 30-lever frame. As can be seen from this view, this is much smaller than the original interlocking and at its far end has a green IFS control panel. This regulates traffic in Harborough on the main Barnetby to Grimsby passenger line.

RIGHT: *Wrawby Junction*: The 137-lever box at Wrawby Junction has thankfully been listed by English Heritage. It is the largest single-manned box on the network and controls the signals at Wrawby Junction, which have become one of the best recognised railway locations in the country. This view, taken from the Lincoln line, shows a Cleethorpes to Newark Northgate train passing the imposing structure. Built in 1916 by the Great Central Railway, it is due to close in 2016, in its centenary year. An excellent interior view taken by signaller John Illingworth is found in chapter 11 of this book, illustrating the unusual numbering of the 137 levers, A to E, then 1-131.

FEATURED LINES
YORK TO HARROGATE

Since the resignalling of the line between Sleaford and Spalding, this line is perhaps the most expensive line in the country to operate if one compares passenger revenue to manning costs. What do these two lines have in common – manual gated crossings. Level crossing safety is a priority for Network Rail and after several high-profile fatalities, there is a drive to reduce the number of level crossings and where this is not feasible provide as safe a crossing as possible. Behind the drive for crossing safety is a little-recognised fact that Network Rail has to contend with. In the UK, it is assumed that if there is a fatality on the railway, it is Network Rail's fault for not protecting its property with pallisade fencing and locked gates more suited to a category B prison. Yet just across the channel and over the Atlantic, the assumption is that if somebody trespasses on the railway and is injured, it is their fault. Thus open crossings on secondary lines are commonplace throughout Europe and fencing is unheard of in Germany, Austria and Switzerland. In the USA, 10,000-ton container trains thunder past at 70mph with no fencing and just a warning light on most rural crossings. In this setting, many secondary lines in the UK still have gated crossings on farm tracks and little used byways which require staff to look after them, often for two or three shifts a day. The line from York to Harrogate is fascinating as it has 10 such crossings in just 20 miles of line.

ABOVE: *Poppleton*: Dating back to the early 1870s, Poppleton signal box is of wooden construction and is really little more than a garden shed. It contains an 11-lever frame and in 2007 benefited from the addition of toilet and kitchen facilities. In 2008, Black 5 No. 45231 departs with the 'Scarborough Spa Express'. Amazingly, the signalman on duty didn't seem to mind about the photographers on the tracks, but was obsessed with shouting at me when I was standing on the flowerbed in an old railway truck in the car park, well out of harm's way!

ABOVE: *Hammerton*: The signal box at Hammerton station is unique on the network as it is housed in a platform cupboard. Built in 1972, the cupboard contains the original 1914, 10-lever frame. At the end of the late shift, the cupboard is locked up and then reopened when the early turn comes to work the next morning. The block token instruments, and facilities such as the signallers' kitchen, are in the old station buildings a couple of yards away. Although it is just less than four miles from Hammerton station to Cattal in the west, there is another manned crossing between them at Hammerton Road. Similarly, the six-mile stretch to Poppleton in the east has another two manned crossings.

ABOVE: *Harrogate*: Class 150 No. 150270 approaches Harrogate on April 2, 2014, with a train from York. The large gantry and derelict ground are a reminder of the once extensive layout here. Harrogate signal box, which controls the station area, was built in 1947 and today has a 45-lever frame, reduced in size with just levers 21-65 still present in the box.

ABOVE: *Hessay:* Hessay manual gated crossing, between Hammerton and Poppleton, is controlled from a ground frame seen here. The station is long closed and converted to a private dwelling, but the crossing is still manned for 18 hours a day.

BELOW: *Belmont Crossing*: Class 150 No. 150205 recedes with a York to Leeds via Harrogate train, which has just crossed the busy road at Belmont. The box here was built by the NE railway in 1914 and has a 1968-installed five-lever frame.

YORK-HARROGATE – 2014

ABOVE: *Starbeck*: This used to be an important junction, where the direct line north to Ripon and Northallerton left the Harrogate to York route. When it closed in 1962, the frame in this 915 NE box was reduced from 51 to 26 levers. Here, in 1988, a Harrogate to York train approaches from the west.

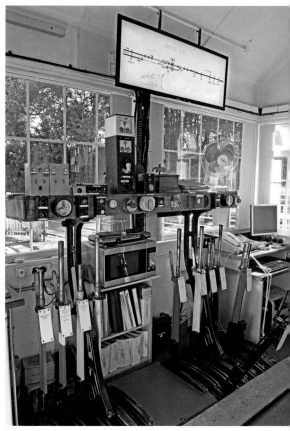

ABOVE AND RIGHT: *Cattal*: The signaller at Cattal closes the gates on the quiet country road that crosses the tracks here. The signal box was built in 1892 and contains a 16-lever frame. The interior view shows where some of the levers were removed in the 1960s when the goods yard was closed. Cattal station stands next to The Victoria, one of the best pub restaurants in Yorkshire.

ABOVE: *Marston Moor*: The restored 1910 signal box here guards the second of the manned crossings between Hammerton and Poppleton. It contains a 16-lever frame, but since singling of the line it is no longer a block post, the section now stretching the six miles from Poppleton to Hammerton.

BELOW: *Knaresborough*: Glimpsed from the passing train, the unusual signal box at Knaresborough is built onto the terrace of houses next to the station. The 1873 signal box contains a 12-lever frame and the signaller also mans the gated crossing seen in this view.

ABOVE: *Hammerton Road*: The gated crossing at Hammerton Road between Hammerton and Cattal is rarely used. It is difficult to justify two or even three crossing keepers' salaries for just a handful of cars and farm vehicles, but such are the HSE pressures and the assumption of guilt placed on Network Rail that a common sense continental approach to quiet country crossings like this has been impossible to implement.

ABOVE: *Whixley Crossing*: The crossing keeper at Whixley pops out of his cabin on a dreary day in May 2014 to ask if I want the gates open for my car. I assure him I am just using the foot crossing and taking a couple of pictures at this rarely visited spot.

East Anglia

The Romford ROC has its origins in the Crossrail project. Due to open in 2015, the ROC is sited in Romford, largely because all the Network Rail land adjacent to Stratford was used up for the Olympics. Originally planned as a Network Management Centre in the days of Railtrack, it is sited on almost the last bit of Network Rail land to the east of London, but inside the M25.

While it is situated in the corner of East Anglia, it will eventually control all the railway in Essex, Suffolk, Norfolk and Cambridgeshire, interfacing with the York ROC for much of its western boundary.

HISTORICAL SCHEME

CAMBRIDGE AND ELY

Resignalling in the Cambridge area started in 1977 when the newly opened King's Cross panel box reached as far as Royston on February 5, 1977. Then in October 1982, the Cambridge power signal box opened. On October 17 the boxes at Cambridge South (128 levers),

Cambridge North (70 levers) and Coldhams Lane Junction (85 levers) were closed.

That same week on October 20 the signal box at Whittlesford burnt down and was replaced by a temporary manual signal box which was eventually absorbed into Cambridge panel in September 1983. In the interim Shepreth Branch Junction and Shepreth station joined the panel in February 1983, followed by Fulbourne and Six Mile Bottom on the Newmarket line in May 1983.

Finally in September 1983 Shelford Junction closed, followed by Great Chesterford in December 1983. It was then in November 1984 that Chesterton Junction and Waterbeach closed.

The incorporation of the Ely area into Cambridge power box did not take place until 1992. On April 11, 1992, Soham, Ely Dock Junction and Ely North & South closed. A couple of weeks later, on April 27, 1992, Ely North Junction closed. From here the panel fringed with manual signalling on all three lines north and it was not until 2012 that the Ely to Norwich line was added to the panel. The lines to King's Lynn and Peterborough remain manually signalled.

LEFT AND TOP: *Coldhams Lane Junction:* Taken in 1978, this monochrome view shows the signal diagram at Coldhams Lane Junction. From the box steps, on May 6, 1981, Class 03 No. 37036 is checked on the Newmarket lines with the morning trip back from Newmarket to Cambridge yard. The consist of the freight is made up of two vacuum-fitted grain wagons to Muir of Ord and air-braked Polybulks to Barry and Birkenhead Docks. The addition of tracks and point work for the Cambridge diesel depot led to significant expansion of the box at Coldhams Lane in 1959, with a total of 85 levers in the frame at the time of this photograph.

LEFT: *Cambridge North and Coldhams Lane Junction:* One of the best vantage points for the signals to the north of Cambridge station was Mill Road bridge. Here, in March 1979, Class 40 No. 40124 passes from the control of Coldhams Lane box (visible above the middle of the train), to Cambridge North.
The train is 8J21, the lunchtime Whitemoor to Temple Mills mixed freight.

YEAR	BOXES TRANSFERRED
2015	Anglian integrated control centre, Romford electrical control, Upminster IECC
2016	Acle, Brundall Junction, Brundall XGP, Cantley, Chapel Road XGF, Lingwood XGF, Lowestoft, Oulton Broad North, Reedham Junction, Strumpshaw XG, Yarmouth Vauxhall
2017	Bury St Edmunds, Cambridge PSB, Chippenham Junction, Colchester PSB, Crown Point, Dullingham, Elsenham Crossing, Foxton XGB, Parkeston
2018	Acton Canal Wharf, Acton Wells Junction, Dudding Hill Junction, Neasden Junction, Richmond, South Tottenham, Upper Holloway, Stowmarket XGB
2019	Inganestone XGB, Liverpool Street IECC
2020	Kings Dyke, Manea, March East, March South, Stonea, Three Horse Shoes
2021	Downham Market, King's Lynn Junction, Littleport, Magdalen Road, Whittlesea, Whittlesea XGP
2022	Saxmundham
2030	Trowse Swing Bridge (TBC)
2034	Deep Wharf XGP, Jurgens XGP
2038	Lincoln Road XGP, Park Lane XGP, Trinity Lane XGP
2044	Clacton PSB
2051	Reedham, Oulton Broad and Somerleyton Swing Bridges (note this may change as the swing bridges are life expired and may need replacing before 2051)

ABOVE: *Cambridge:* Cambridge Power Signal box: Taken in September 1983, the area covered by the Cambridge panel can clearly be seen in this picture. With Cambridge station in the middle the lines to Newmarket and Waterbeach can be seen to the right of the image and those to Royston and Great Chesterford to the left.

Cambridge South: Cambridge South was the largest signal box in the Cambridge area with 128 levers. Class 37 No. 37092 accelerates past the box with the 17.26, Cambridge to London Liverpool express on April 30, 1981. This was a red letter day as the afternoon produced Class 20 Nos. 20159 & 20142 on 8J93, the afternoon freight from March Whitemoor to Temple Mills yard. The locomotives worked through to London that afternoon.

TOP RIGHT: *Cambridge North*: The 70-lever Cambridge North box closed on October 17, 1982, demolished shortly thereafter. On October 12, 1979, a Class 31 is seen diverging into the yard at Cambridge with the return of the morning trip to Newmarket and the Fulbourbe Blue Circle cement works. The traffic on this day is empty MCO coal wagons from there with a guards van at each end because of the track layout at Fulbourne.

RIGHT: A second image from a similar vantage point in February 1980, shows Class 31 No. 31019 passing the box with 8J21, the lunch time March Whitemoor to Temple Mills mixed freight. This was one of three or four such services each day in the late 1970s and 1980, which took unfitted traffic into London, avoiding slow trains on the East Coast Main Line and also the Midland Main Line.

LEFT: *Chesterton Junction*: In May 1980, the driver of Class 37 No. 37090 hands the token for the single line to Fen Drayton to the signalman at Chesterton Junction. He is leaving the branch with the daily (8B45) Fen Drayton to King's Cross sand train. Much of the branch is now part of the Cambridge bus-way. The signal box closed in November 1984.

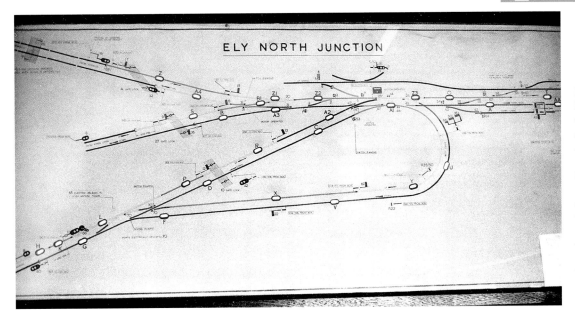

ELY NORTH JUNCTION

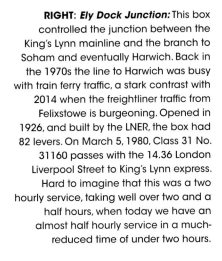

LEFT: Ely North Junction: Ely is known as the 'Crewe of the east' and its epicentre is Ely North Junction. Back in the 1970s and 80s, the two hourly Norwich to Birmingham expresses avoided Ely station as did freights from Norwich, Brandon and King's Lynn to Whitemoor, all using the avoiding line at Ely North. The box here (signal diagram, photographed in 1979), was built in 1926 and had 76 levers. Fast forward to September 1987 and Class 37 No. 37215 passes the box with 6N64, the Duxford to Tyne yard Speedlink service. The train was organised in this way because of the chemical traffic from Duxford to Teeside and crucially the traffic of glue from Duxford to the chipboard factory in Hexham.

RIGHT: *Ely Dock Junction:* This box controlled the junction between the King's Lynn mainline and the branch to Soham and eventually Harwich. Back in the 1970s the line to Harwich was busy with train ferry traffic, a stark contrast with 2014 when the freightliner traffic from Felixstowe is burgeoning. Opened in 1926, and built by the LNER, the box had 82 levers. On March 5, 1980, Class 31 No. 31160 passes with the 14.36 London Liverpool Street to King's Lynn express. Hard to imagine that this was a two hourly service, taking well over two and a half hours, when today we have an almost half hourly service in a much-reduced time of under two hours.

LEFT: *Ely North:* Ely station boasted two signal boxes, north and south. Ely South had a 75-lever frame, compared to Ely North, seen here, which had a 41-lever frame in a 1880-built box. Class 37 No. 37021 passes Ely North signal box on June 10, 1982, with a King's Lynn to London Liverpool Street express.

RIGHT: *Whittlesford*: Class 37 No. 37118, hauling the 11.52 Cambridge to London Liverpool Street express, passes Whittlesford signal box in February 1982, shortly before it burnt down.

THE WHERRY LINES – 2014

[Map of the Wherry Lines showing: To Cromer, Norwich, To Diss, To Ely, Whittlingham Junction, Brundall Crossing, Brundall, Lingwood, Lingwood Crossing, Chapel Road Crossing, Acle, Yarmouth, Cantley, Reedham Swing Bridge, Reedham Junction, Somerleyton Swing Bridge, Oulton Broad North, Lowestoft, To Ipswich, Oulton Broad Swing Bridge]

FEATURED LINES
THE WHERRY LINES

Since the incorporation of the Ely signal boxes into the Cambridge power box in 1992, East Anglia saw relatively little change in the signalling infrastructure until 2012 when the manual boxes between Ely and Norwich were closed. The next few years will see large areas of manual signalling from Bury St Edmunds to Peterborough and Ely to King's Lynn phased out. Another outpost of Victorian signalling controls, the routes from Norwich to Yarmouth and Lowestoft are known as the Wherry lines. The boxes along these routes are due to close in 2016.

ABOVE: *Brundall Crossing*: Situated between the up and down platforms at Brundall station is a manual gated crossing, separately manned from the main signal box 200 yards further east. This arrangement is mirrored elsewhere in East Anglia at Whittlesford. In April 2003 the signaller reopens the gates for traffic to and from the Broomes boat yard and the local pub.

RIGHT: *Acle*: There is a long history of locomotive haulage on summer Saturdays on the route to Yarmouth and more recently two trains each day have run through from Liverpool Street on summer Saturdays. Built in 1883 to a GE design, the box contains the original 1883, 20-lever frame, seen here in 2012.

ABOVE: *Brundall*: More typical motive power for the 'Yarmouth Drags' is Class 47 No. 47714 accelerating past Brundall station in 2006. The signal box here dates from 1883 and contains a 35-lever frame. The line to the left is the direct route to Yarmouth, via Acle. The afternoon Yarmouth to London has travelled via Reedham Junction.

ABOVE: *Cantley*: The signaller at Cantley has a manual crossing to look after as well as controlling trains along the mainline to Lowestoft. Freight traffic to the adjacent sugar factory is sadly a thing of the past, so many of the 22 levers in the 1887-era cabin are white or unused.

RIGHT: *Chapel Road Crossing*: There are two manual crossings in Lingwood, both manned 24 hours a day. To the west of the station is Chapel Road crossing, where the crossing keeper has a white metal temporary building as accommodation.

ABOVE: *Lowestoft*: Signalman Chris Ashling stands beneath the box diagram in Lowestoft signal box. With the terminus station and extensive goods yard, the box is the second largest on the Wherry lines with 61 levers. Only Yarmouth is bigger with 63 levers, but more of those are out of use than in Lowestoft.

RIGHT: *Oulton Broad North*: This view of a Norwich to Lowestoft service shows Oulton Broad North Junction with the line to Ipswich diverging to the left. The signal box at Oulton Broad North controls this junction, although it is on the Norwich line. The 1901 box has a 35-lever frame, which was expanded in 1928 to cover control of the junction here.

LEFT: *Reedham Junction*: Class 47 No. 47810 approaches Reedham station with a Yarmouth to London summer Saturday extra. Built in 1904, the signal box here has 60 levers and controls the junction to Berney arms and Yarmouth.

TOP LEFT: *Reedham Swing Bridge*: The water jets have been turned off as Class 57 Nos. 57306 and 57310 haul the RHTT over Reedham Swing Bridge in October 2012. The signal box was built to a GE design in 1904 and contains a 12-lever frame as well as the control mechanism for the swing bridge. Both Reedham and Somerleyton still use paraffin lamps for the warning lights on the bridges and these are perhaps the last four lamps left on the network that still use paraffin. The bridges are swung by a series of wires and pulleys and these Victorian-designed mechanisms are in need of refurbishment. It is still not clear whether refurbishment or replacement of these wonderful bridges is the best way forward, and there is therefore no clear date for the closure of the signal boxes attached to them.

LEFT: In May 2013, Michael Barnett from Clacton changes the lamps on Reedham Swing Bridge, two of four remaining. The signals along the Lowestoft line lost their lamps 18 months earlier and just nine months earlier the warning lights on local level crossings were converted to LED bulbs. Michael also delivers mail for everybody along the line from Saxmundham to Norwich and undertakes minor repairs along the route. Another duty is to unlock the points at Yarmouth on summer Saturdays when the station sees extra traffic. On duty in the signal box that day was Alan English who starred alongside Michael Portillo when he visited the line and watched the swing bridge in operation. Between April 2012 and April 2013 the bridge was swung 1472 times, an average of nearly five times a day.

ABOVE AND LEFT: *Yarmouth*: The winter sun catches the windows of Yarmouth signal box. For a short spell in 1999, fertiliser was carried from Harwich to Yarmouth by rail and unloaded in the old carriage sidings to the west of the station. Class 37 No. 37242 shunts the wagons in the station on January 11, 1999, having arrived as 6G10 from Harwich. The signal box dates from 1884, but the 63-lever frame is more modern, having been installed in 1905. Rationalisation at the once-busy seaside station has led to a few gaps in the frame as well as 24 white disused levers.

East Midlands

ABOVE: *Leicester*. A busy scene at the north end of Leicester in June 1980. Class 45 No. 45105 heads north with a Sheffield bound express, while Class 45 No. 45069 is checked on the 'up' slow line. Leicester North signal box dates from 1911 and was a Midland Type 4c box with 65 levers, sadly now consigned to history. The new power signal box was built roughly where the Class 08 shunting locomotive is seen at the top right hand corner of this image.

ABOVE RIGHT: *Syston*: The box at Syston North dated back to 1891 and was a Midland Railway 3a design with 37 levers. It is seen here, to good effect, on May 19, 1983, as Class 37s Nos. 37079 and 37096 pass with the daily Lackenby to Corby steel coil train.

The Derby ROC will be developed from the East Midlands Signalling Centre to the south of Derby station. Opened in August 2008, the first lines to be controlled from Derby were between Trowell Junction and Clay Cross Junction with the route to Tapton Junction through Chesterfield added in September 2008.

In 2009 the line from Trent Junction to Attenborough was taken over by Derby and in 2011 the Robin Hood line from Nottingham to Kirby Summit moved to the box. This involved the closure of the 'Robin Hood Line' panel in Trent power box. In January 2012 Leicester power box, opened in 1986, was decommissioned with control of the Midland mainline to Wellingborough and the branch to Nuneaton moving to the ROC.

Over the Easter period of 2013, a six week engineering possession saw Nottingham station remodelled and resignalled under the control of Derby, leading to the closure of one of the original power signal boxes left on the network at Trent Junction. The new East Midlands ROC will eventually border the Rugby and Manchester ROCs along its western border and the York ROC to the east.

YEAR	BOXES TRANSFERRED
2011	Kirkby Summit
2012	Croft, Leicester PSB
2013	Netherfield Junction, Rectory Junction, Sneiton GB, Trent PSB
2014	Bingham, Bottesford West Junction, Fiskerton station, Lowdham, Staythorpe Crossing
2015	Manton Junction, Fiskerton Junction, Rolleston station
2016	Derby PSB, Caverswall, Eggington Junction, Foley Crossing, Hilton GC, Scropton, Sudbury, Tutbury Crossing, Uttoxeter
2017	Ashwell, Frisby, Ketton, Langham Junction, Melton station, Oakham Crossing, Uffington, Whissendine, Wyfordby GC, Wymondham GC
2018	Sheffield PSB
2021	Bardon Hill, Mantle Lane, Moira West Junction
2022	Totley Tunnel East
2026	Kiveton Park, Worksop (part of)
2027	Clipstone, Elmton & Cresswell, Maltby Colliery, Norwood, Shirebrook Junction, Thoresby Colliery, Tinsley yard

London Road: In July 1985 an unidentified Class 31 passes London Road signal box with a Norwich to Birmingham New Street service. London Road was a relatively modern LMS box, dating from 1936, with 50 levers.

HISTORICAL SCHEMES

THE 'LEICESTER GAP'

The last main line into London to be controlled by semaphore signals was the Midland route from Leicester to St Pancras. Trent power box opened in September 1969 and controlled routes north from Loughborough but it was not until the end of 1979 that West Hampstead power box was opened at the south end of the Midland man line.

Initially it took control of an area previously covered by Elstree, Harpenden Junction, Harpenden North & South, Luton North & South, Napsbury, Radlett, and St.Albans South signal boxes. In June 1980, the signal boxes at Bedford Junction, Bedford North, Flitwick, Harlington, Kempston Road Junction, Laegrave and Millbrooks all closed, as the panel at West Hampstead extended its reach northwards.

In April 1981 the complex area around Cricklewood and Brent yards was resignalled with the closure of Brent Junction, Cricklewood Junction, Engine shed Junction, Finchley Road and Hendon boxes. A month later in May 1981, the Hampstead panel was extended north with closure of Sharnbrook box.

In July 1982 the Westinghouse OCS panel at St Pancras was closed with control of the terminus moved to West Hampstead. There was then a pause and semaphore signalling continued to control the Midland main line from north of Sharnbrook to Loughborough and around this time the phrase 'The Leicester Gap' was christened. It was not until the end of June 1986 that Leicester itself was resignalled and control of the area transferred to a new power signal box utilising an NX panel and sited adjacent to the locomotive depot in Leicester.

This initially took over from the manual boxes at Bell Lane, Desford Colliery Sidings, Kibworth station, Kilby

Knighton South Junction: With the signalman conveniently silhouetted in the open door, Class 31 No. 31414 speeds past Knighton South Junction with a Birmingham New Street express. The service ran for many years every two hours, only to be effectively replaced by the now hourly Cambridge to Birmingham service, which often struggles for capacity in the three-coach DMU deployed on the service. Knighton South is again a fairly modern LMSR box, dating from 1935 and having 60 levers.

Bridge, Knighton South Junction, Leicester North, Little Bowden Junction, London Road Junction, Market Harborough No.3, Wigston North & South Junctions and Wistow.

This transfer of control occurred at the end of June 1986 and was followed by abolition of semaphore signals on the mainline in Deceber 1987 when the boxes at Finedon Road, Glendon North Junction, Irchester South, Kettering station, Loughborough, Neilsons Sidings, Sileby Syston North and South Junctions and Wellingborough station were all taken over by the Leicester power box.

The power box was to have a relatively short life and closed on December 31, 2011, when all its responsibilities were absorbed into the East Midlands ROC at Derby.

LEFT: *Bell Lane (Leicester)*: On a dull day in summer 1985, an HST powers past Bell Lane signal box. The station platform of Leicester can be seen between the HST headed for Sheffield and 31237, which is in the distance on 8E27 the Croft quarry to Leyton ballast. The box was built in 1891 to a Midland Railway No. 2 design, but its frame of 43 levers dated from much more recently in 1959 and was a standard LM frame.

Finedon Road & Neilson Sidings (Wellingborough): This view, taken in June 1983, shows the marshalling yard at Wellingborough. In the foreground, Class 31s Nos. 31294 & 31171 pass Finedon Road signal box with an 'up' stone train. The box at Finedon Road dates from 1893 and had 55 levers. It was among the last boxes to be closed along this line. In the background, Class 47 No. 47362 is almost passing Neilson Sidings box, seen to the right of the train, with an empty oil train returning to Humberside. Neilson Siding was a 20-lever box, dating from the late 19th century, when coal traffic dictated a major staging yard in Wellingborough, and there were coal trains more than once an hour to the capital.

LEFT: *Wellingborough*: The very last bit of the 'gap' was at Wellingborough and didn't get resignalled until December 1987. Here, in July 1979, Class 45 No. 45128 speeds past with a Nottingham to St Pancras express, while Class 45 No. 45077 stands on the slow lines with a cement train from Northfleet to Toton. The box here was a Midland type 2b, dating from 1893, and with 48 levers. It closed on December 6, 1987.

BELOW: *Ashwell*: Class 66 No. 66614 passes Ashwell with 6L87 the Earles to Purfleet cement service, which on August 8, 2011, was loaded to 36 wagons with a trailing weight of 1796 tons. The box at Ashwell opened in 1912 and has 25 levers. It was sympathetically restored in 2005 with uPVC windows which have kept the Midland pattern frames.

FEATURED LINE
LEICESTER TO PETERBOROUGH

This cross country route between Leicester and Peterborough has assumed increased importance since it was cleared for continental loading gauge containers and designated part of the core freight Network. On top of the hourly Cambridge to Birmingham service, there is an increasing volume of freight traffic along the route which remains manually signalled from Frisby in the west to Uffington & Barnack in the east.

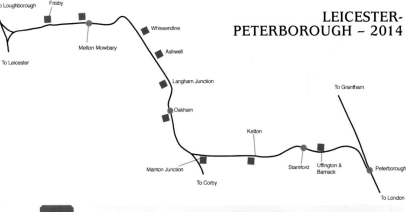

LEICESTER-PETERBOROUGH – 2014

Frisby: In contrast to Ashwell box, the modernisation of Frisby has radically altered the appearance of the 1941-built box. The small, 10-lever frame was replaced by an IFS panel in 1987; it fringed with Leicester power box when this view was taken in 2011.

Langham Junction: The immaculate 20-lever Midland tumbler frame at Langham Junction is kept polished by resident signaller Jon Ward. The box, opened in 1890, is called 'junction' in keeping with the Midland practice of calling a box that controlled access to passing loops a junction. The signal diagram (**left**) clearly shows the passing loops, which run as far as Oakham station. Class 37 No. 97301 (**above**) passes Langham Junction in June 2011 with 1Q52, a test train from Derby to St Pancras. The passing loops which start here may have seemed redundant for the last couple of decades since the cessation of direct London services via Corby and the closure of the steelworks at Corby, but with the planned increase in container traffic it may proved a wise decision not to have removed them in the 1980s.

LEFT AND BELOW: *Manton Junction*: Back in 1983, Class 31 No. 31121 passes Manton Junction with 1E64 a Birmingham New Street to Norwich express. At this time the 1913-built London Midland cabin contained a 35-lever manual frame. By the time of my visit in 2013, two new NX panels had been installed controlling the cross-country route and the line south past Corby. These were installed in 1988 and 1998.

TOP AND ABOVE: *Melton station:* On April 11, 2011, Class 20 Nos. 20901 & 20905 head new Metropolitan line stock through Melton station. Class 20 Nos. 20227 & 20142 are propelling the train, which has run round in the passing loops to the east of Melton Mowbray and will now head back west as 7X09 the Old Dalby to Amersham working. The signal box at Melton was built in 1942 with a 45-lever frame. Added to this in 1978 was an NX panel to control Brettingby Junction at the east end of the passing loops to the east of the station. A second NX panel was added in 1986 to control access to the Pedigree Petfoods factory. While no longer rail served, the IFS panel still controls access to the 'down' passing loop.

A second view of Melton station shows the remains of the once extensive goods yard here. Class 60 No. 60074 passes with 6M67 an empty stone train from Broxbourne to Mountsorrel.

ABOVE AND LEFT: *Oakham*: The level crossing is famous as the prototype model for Hornby's first model of a signal box. Built in 1899 it has a 17-lever frame, seen here with 'Pinkie', one of the longest-serving signallers in the area, chatting to the signaller from Ashwell, Adrian Quine. The red coffee pot dates back to when Pinkie started on the railway 40 years earlier, as does his transport to work, a BSA Bantam motorbike.
Class 66 No. 66722 passes Oakham on September 16, 2011, with 4L22 the Hams Hall to Felixstowe container train. The opening of the new Ipswich chord and clearance of the Peterborough to Nuneaton route for continental gauge containers should see a marked rise in this type of train along the line.

RIGHT: *Uffington*: Signaller Duncan Pike opens the gates at Uffington in August 2011. The box opened in 1909 and has a 16-lever frame.

FEATURED SIGNAL BOX

Uttoxeter: The signal box here could perhaps lay claim to being the last built manual signal box in the UK, having opened with 40 levers in 1981. That same year a new 16-lever manual box was opened at Porth in the Rhondda Valley, but while the frame was altered for the job in Porth, it was housed in a temporary building; therefore, the box at Uttoxeter can claim to be the last purpose-built manual signal box on the network. Here, in February 2012, Class 153 No. 153308 passes with a Crewe to Derby service. The extensive signalling reflects the former sidings at Uttoxeter, now long gone.

RIGHT: ***Whissendine***: East Midlands Trains started running a Derby to St Pancras service via Melton and Corby and it is seen here in 2011 passing Whissendine box. Opened in 1940 and with a 20-lever frame, the recently installed uPVC windows look a little out of place in the box.

Southern Region

T he Southern Region is perhaps the place in the UK with the least manual signalling, and this chapter reflects that situation. As things stand at the end of 2014, there will be four ROCs on the southern at Ashford, Gillingham, Three Bridges and Basingstoke. The signalling centre at Ashford opened in 1993 and is an IECC panel controlling HS1 and it is likely looking ahead that this will remain its sole purpose. As far as Kent and Sussex are concerned, it is likely that the old North Kent Signalling Centre at Gillingham will be incorporated into the newly built Three Bridges ROC. Certainly there is a drive to merge the Kent and Sussex routes. As for Basingstoke, the current signal box here dates back to 1966 and the electrification of the Southampton route that saw the demise of the mighty Bullied Pacifics. A new building is under construction and this will control the west of the region.

FEATURED LINES
HORSHAM TO LITTLEHAMPTON AND BOGNOR REGIS

BELOW: *Amberley*:
The Mid-Sussex line boxes from Bilingshurst to Amberley closed on March 14, 2014, with control moved to the Three Bridges ROC. In June 2013, London Victoria to Bognor Regis services cross at Amberley, which had a particularly fine slotted home signal still in use. Signaller Jason Greenfield was on duty in the tiny 1950s-built wooden cabin with its 1934 vintage 14-lever frame. Prior to the construction of the wooden cabin on the platform, the frame was out in the open. The signallers' quarters here are part of the old station buildings with a hatch to the outside, which was used as a post box in former times as well as to sell tickets (a job done by the signalman in the past).

YEAR	BOXES TRANSFERRED
2013	Berwick, Eastbourne, Hampden Park, Pevensey, Polegate, Havensmouth, Plumpton XGB, Bexhill
2014	Amberley, Billingshurst, Pullborough
2015	Arundel, Barnham, Chichester, Littlehampton, Lewes, Newhaven Harbour, Newhaven Town
2016	Lancing, Victoria SCC (part of)
2017	Lovers Walk depot panel, Three Bridges PSB (part of)
2018	London Bridge PSB, Angerstein
2019	Whyteleafe South XGB, Bounds Green North shunt box, Bounds Green south shunt box, King's Cross PSB (transfer over three years)
2020	Victoria SCC
2021	Cricklewood shunt box
2022	Oxted, West Hampstead PSB
2023	Selhurst depot panel
2057	Bognor Regis Basingstoke ROC
2012	Chard Junction, Gillingham Dorset, Honiton, Templecombe, Yeovil Junction, Feniton XGP, Sherborne XGP
2014	Aldershot, Farnham, Ash Vale Junction, Hamworthy Junction, Poole, Wareham, Wool, Stoke XG
2016	Dorchester South, Yeovil Pen Mill
2017	Salisbury
2018	Basingstoke ASC, Eastleigh PSB, Farncombe, Feltham, Guildford PSB, Haslemere, Petersfield, Woking, Wokingham
2019	Wimbledon SCC, Wimbledon Top yard depot panel, Clapham yard
2023	Brockenhurst, Marchwood, School Road MGH
2029	Bournemouth
2035	Havant ASC
2040	Dorking

GILLINGHAM ROC

YEAR	BOXES TRANSFERRED
(NB it is anticipated this ROC will be merged into Three Bridges ROC in 2019)	
2011	Canterbury East, Shepherds Well, Faversham, Margate, Ramsgate
2012	Snodland
2015	Gillingham, Rainham, Rochester, Sittingbourne
2017	Deal, Minster, Sandwich
2019	Ashford IECC (north Kent), Slade Green depot panel, Ashford-Hoo Junction, Ashford-Dartford West

ASHFORD ROC

YEAR	BOXES TRANSFERRED
(changes subject to decision as to the size of Three Bridges)	
2016	Maidstone East
2017	Folkestone East
2018	Tonbridge
2019	Wye area control centre
2047	Canterbury West, Sturry
2048	Bopeep Junction
2053	Hastings, Robertsbridge, Rye
2055	Aylesford, Cuxton, East Farleigh, Wateringbury, Maidstone West

RIGHT AND BELOW: *Bognor Regis*: While there were three manual boxes surviving between Amberley and Billingshurst, the boxes at Arundel and Horsham (Littlehaven) at either end of the Mid-Sussex line were, respectively, a small NX panel (1979) and an IFS panel (2012). At the southern end of the line, however, are two pockets of semaphore signalling in Bognor Regis and Littlehampton. In June 2013, local area manager Brian Anderson chats to Trevor Maxted (signaller from Guildford). Built in 1938, the box has a 65-lever frame. Class 377 No.377464 passes the box with a Victoria service on June 10, 2013.

***Billingshurst*:** Billingshurst signal box is the oldest-surviving signal box on the southern region and the only surviving example of the earliest Saxby & Farmer design. While the frame dates from 1876, the box itself is probably from earlier (between 1866 and 1868). The box is listed and after closure in 2014 was to be moved to the Amberley museum. In 2013, signaller Paul Charman is working the 19-lever Saxby & Farmer frame.

ABOVE AND RIGHT:
Littlehampton:
The compact London Brighton and South Coast Railway box at Littlehampton was opened in 1886 and only just has room for the 44-lever frame, which extends right up to the retaining walls. Signaller Mark Crouch update his emails during our visit in June 2013. The box is tucked back from the track and hardly visible from the station, although the terminus does boast a fine array of semaphores. Class 377 No. 377415 arrives with London Victoria service in June 2013.

ABOVE AND BELOW: *Pulborough*: The 1878 box at Pulborough is another of the earlier Saxby & Farmer designs, built for the London Brighton & South Coast Railway, and with a 30-lever frame. During our visit in 2013, signaller John Spears discussed the finer points of Southern Region signalling with us in a box, which had recently been repainted and was in excellent exterior condition, as can be seen from the view of Class 377 No. 377441 with a Victoria to Bognor service.

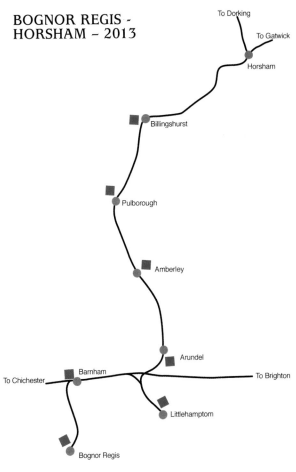

BOGNOR REGIS - HORSHAM – 2013

To Dorking

To Gatwick

Horsham

Billingshurst

Pulborough

Amberley

Arundel

To Chichester · Barnham · To Brighton

Littlehamptom

Bognor Regis

FEATURED LINES
POOLE TO WOOL

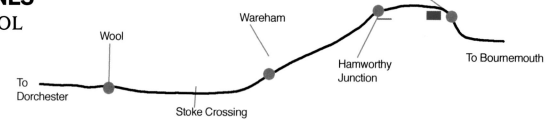

ABOVE: *Hamworthy Junction*: Local manager and railway author Mark Jamieson 'takes the token' from Trevor Maxted in Hamworthy box – Trevor is messing around as usual. Hamworthy Junction controlled the branch down to the docks, now mothballed, but used for steel in the 1990s. Built in 1893 it has a 59-lever frame; most levers in the frame are, however, white and out of use.

RIGHT: *Stoke Crossing*: Crossing keeper Simon Keiper maintains a watchful eye as a tractor crosses the Weymouth to Bournemouth mainline at Stoke, between Wool and Wareham. Manual crossings such as this are an extremely expensive luxury on today's railways.

ABOVE AND LEFT: *Poole*: Signaller Mark Cooper searches for an image of Poole from steam days during a quiet spell in Poole signal box. The box dates from 1897 and was formerly called Poole West. The 51-lever frame was the result of extension in 1934, but as seen in this view several of the levers have been removed, while others are out of use.

Back in 1983, 4-VEP EMU No. 406 approaches Poole propelled by Class 33 No. 33104 with a Weymouth to Waterloo service. In the background Class 33 No. 33101 is looped with 6W86, the daily Wool to Eastleigh Speedlink service, while Class 47 No. 47515 is in the carriage sidings with what will be a Poole to Leeds cross country train.

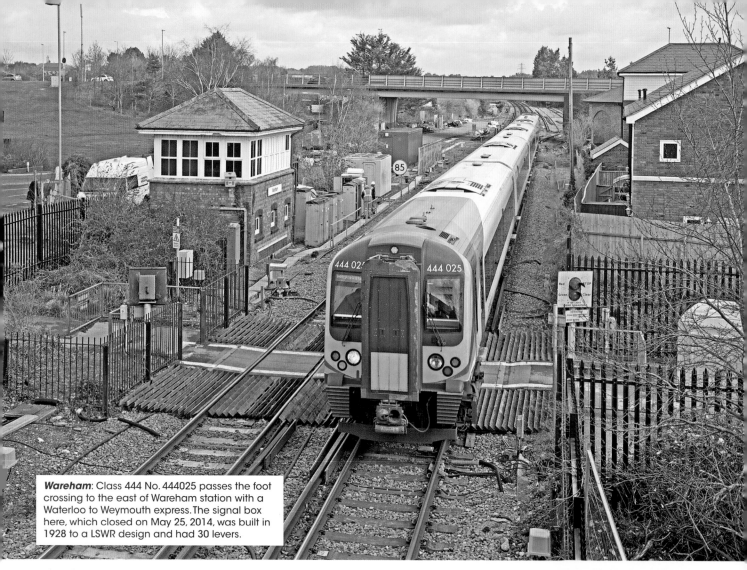

Wareham: Class 444 No. 444025 passes the foot crossing to the east of Wareham station with a Waterloo to Weymouth express. The signal box here, which closed on May 25, 2014, was built in 1928 to a LSWR design and had 30 levers.

ABOVE AND RIGHT: *Wool*: The compact 19-lever frame at Wool is well seen here as signaller Paul enters data. Built in 1890 the signal box also controlled the crossing to the west of Wool station. Interestingly, as the view of Class 444 No. 444030, shows, refurbishment of the crossing involved the installation of a CCTV system rather than the troublesome radar and LIDAR (low level radar) used in other recent resignalling schemes.

The tale is told of a flock of crows which was feasting on a discarded KFC meal at Eccles Road in Norfolk. They had brought the line to a standstill for several hours as the LIDAR could not scan the crossing as clear of obstructions.

FEATURED SIGNAL BOX

ABOVE AND BELOW: *Hastings*: The second largest remaining manual signal box on the southern region (after Maidstone West) is at Hastings. Built in 1930, it has an 84-lever Westinghouse frame. Signaller Richard Connolly showed us round in June 2013.

Class 377 No. 377420 passes Hastings box with a London Charing Cross to Ore service. while a Class 170 DMU is in the up platform with the Ashford service.

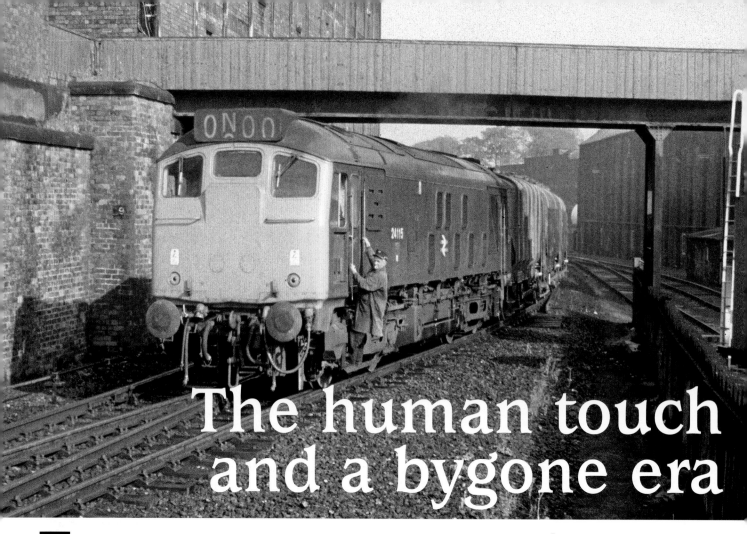

The human touch and a bygone era

TOP: *Cameron Bridge*: Class 24 No. 24115 shunts at Cameron Bridge in 1976. The shunter hangs from the door, fag in mouth, as the CGO grain wagons are hauled from the distillery to be taken back to Thornton yard.

ABOVE LEFT: *Worksop*: Guard Reg Speight holds his trophy aloft in Worksop yard back in 1986. The rabbit was snared at Kiveton Park colliery, while Class 56 No. 56114 (behind him) was eased through the rapid loader at Kiveton Park colliery before departing as 6F39 the morning train to Worksop yard. His yard office colleagues look on with amusement, while in the background are (from left) the rear end of 6T02, a trip from Worksop to Blidworth colliery; 56087 with 6D66, a loaded MGR to Scunthorpe CHP coal terminal (for the steelworks); 37120 with 9T84, a Beighton to Cottam ballast working; and 20098 and 20015 with 6T13 the morning trip to Manton Wood colliery.

I t often seems said that "things were better in the old days"! Forgotten are the hardships of life on the footplate of a steam engine during a freezing winter or roasting summer. Forgotten are the draughty windows of a large signal box and the struggle to keep warm with a pot bellied stove parked in the corner of the cabin. But maybe some things about the Victorian, manually signalled railway were better?

Certainly there was much more freedom for railway staff and signallers to make their own decisions without senior management having any idea what was going on. There was also far less burden from draconian health and safety legislation. Hopefully these incidents from the last 35 years capture a flavour of what is being lost as the people and manual signal boxes they operate disappear from our railway network:

LOST IN METHIL – SCOTTISH BRANCH LINES IN THE 1970s

A freedom of Scotland ticket in 1976 was the catalyst to a visit to every depot and stabling point north of the border.

One particularly difficult location to track down was Methil docks, which was listed as the stabling point for one of the Class 08 shunting locomotives allocated to Dunfermline Townhill depot. Having found all but two of these Fife based shunting locomotives, I caught a bus in Kircaldy, headed for Methil. After wandering around for over an hour in Methil, I found the remains of a once substantial freight yard with Class 24 No. 24115 ticking over next to the errant Class 08, No. 08271. Nobody was to be found in the shunters cabin which sat adjacent to the ground frame controlling access to the yard. I tried the cab of the Class 24 – key in place, fired up and ready to go, but no crew in sight. I decided they must be nearby, so parked my self in the shunter's 'bothy'.

Fifteen minutes later, the crew arrived having had an excellent lunch at the local pub. I explained what I was

doing sitting in their 'bothy' at which they insisted they take me back to Thornton yard from where they could put me on the staff bus to Kirkcaldy at no charge. This, they reasoned, had the advantage of me seeing the last Class 08 on my wish list, No. 08425, which was the yard pilot at Thornton and making it back to Kirkcaldy without charge via Thornton, which was a notoriously difficult location to reach on public transport anyway.

The ride back from Methil was initially as engine and brake van, but we stopped at Cameron Bridge to pick up some empty grain wagons. As a naive school boy I asked how long they got for a lunch break, to be greeted by hoots of laughter as they explained that they'd been in the pub for two hours and had five pints of 'best', something they did most days when they did the Methil trip.

Regaled by numerous stories about life on the footplate from the 1950s and 60s which included breakfast cooked on the fireman's shovel and unscheduled stops to pick blackberries or check on rabbit snares, we arrived back at Thornton yard without incident. Interestingly, a decade later, I arrived at Worksop yard to find the crew of a coal service from Kiveton Park colliery posing in front of their train with a fine rabbit, retrieved from the snares at the colliery while their MGR service had loaded.

THE SLEEPING SIGNALMAN –
ACCESS TO BRITAIN'S SIGNAL BOXES IN THE LAST HALF CENTURY

Access to signal boxes has always been unpredictable. From the outset, these structures have held a fascination for me. It was not however, until the mid-1970s when I was invited up into Radyr Junction one tea time that the bug bit.

I became a regular in the box, but quickly found that while some signallers relished the company and the interest I showed, others were far less welcoming. Further exploration of freight-only lines, most controlled by manual signal boxes, led to many more signal box visits, usually to try and ascertain if there were any trains in the vicinity. A routine thank you after a visit was an 8x10 black and white print of the box sent to the signalman. A considerable amount of effort in those days when compared with the instant emailing of photographs these days.

Over the years many signalmen have thanked me for the prints, but just once the pictures caused problems. The occasion where things didn't work out so well was on a colliery line in the 1980s. I mentioned to the signalman that I'd be delighted to send him a couple of prints of the box, to which he replied that he felt the best view was up the signal about 50 yards away, would I like to go up there for the next train? Delighted I leapt at the chance and was loaned the yellow vest in the box.

The picture came out well – was duly posted to the signalman and then about a year later was published. Over a decade later I revisited the same signal box and asked if we might take a couple of images, only to be met by a very firm rebuttal with mutterings about trespassing and calling the police. My colleague and I beat a hasty retreat, apologising for intruding, but not before the resident signalman shot out a quick question: "You're not that doctor who was here years ago?" – I said that it might be me, why was he asking?

Then the sad tale of my visit in the 1980s came out. Apparently the signalman at the time was known as friendly and welcoming to enthusiasts, friends and family who often had a cup of tea in the box during the many hours of solitude on this quiet colliery line. Indeed, I recollect not only two pots of tea, but also biscuits and cake during my original visit.

Apparently, once my picture had been published with a date specified in the caption, a particularly malicious railway manager had worked out who had been on duty at the time and placed the unfortunate signalman on a final warning for allowing me in the box.

With 40 years unblemished railway service, he was mortified and in the words of the signalman at our later

visit he "was never the same again". So upset was he that he became reclusive and no longer entertained anybody in the box. He retired in his early sixties and died shortly afterwards, scarred by the action of his manager in what was otherwise an unblemished railway career.

Fortunately, the last decade has seen a move away from such dated management attitudes and while safety and efficient running of the railway are paramount, responsible and official visits to these wonderful remnants of a bygone era have once again become possible in many areas. Which brings me to the sleeping signalman...

Back in 1977, I explored the large Great Western signal box at North East Junction, deep in Cardiff's dockland. The 130 lever box had been very busy when East Moors steelworks was in full production, but by summer 1977, the works had closed and very little traffic passed this 130 lever box. With a new Honda 70 moped to aid exploration in South Wales, I headed off to photograph the engine depot at East Moors and wander round the silent and disused steelworks. Finding the signal box, I knocked on the door and climbed the steps to see if there was anybody there. I found the signalman deeply asleep, snoring, with a strong smell of alcohol pervading the afternoon air. I debated whether to wake him, but decided to take a couple of pictures. These were taken using my Practika camera which made a noise like a small bomb going off – the signalman never stirred as the pictures show. Things have changed in the past 40 years but safety standards and particularly drinking on the job is one aspect of the old days which will not be missed.

ABOVE: *Maltby Colliery Sidings*: During my fateful visit in 1986, Class 20 Nos. 20165 and 20150 wind out of Maltby Colliery Sidings with 6Z29, an extra MGR to Toton yard. The box here still controls the access to Maltby and dates back to 1912 when it was built by the Great Central Railway. It has a 36 lever frame and a small panel which controls the Firbeck area.

BELOW FAR LEFT: *North East Junction*: The complex track work of the south end of East Moor steelworks is seen in the diagram of North East Junction signal box.

BELOW LEFT: Most of the splendid 130 lever frame is seen in this interior view of North East Junction signal box. The signalman can be seen sound asleep in the right foreground.

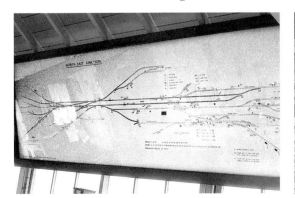

WRONG ROAD MOVEMENT IN THE DAYS BEFORE THE MOBILE PHONE –

A SIGNALMAN'S RECOLLECTIONS

BY TREVOR MAXTED

As a relief signalman I spent four years (1974-1978) covering a vacancy at Victoria Eastern signalbox.

Information and some pictures can be found online at http://tinyurl.com/kfcahby

One summer's evening around 5pm on a late shift, I received the bell code 2-5-5 from the signalman at Stewarts Lane box. This indicated a train running away in the wrong direction. I was puzzled as it is uphill from Stewarts Lane to Victoria and as a rule of thumb trains tend not to run away uphill, so after protecting the line which the 'runaway' would take I made a quick phone call to the Stewarts Lane signalman. "What is going on?" I asked.

It transpired the signalman on duty thought he was signalling a train of empty stock on to the down line. This left Stewarts Lane in the 'up' direction, to then reverse to run ECS to Ramsgate via Factory Junction. The first mistake was the train was in fact empties destined for Victoria. The second error was the driver had taken a new ground signal thinking he was right away to the eastern side of Victoria station. The signalling had been altered the previous weekend and there was obviously confusion as to the meaning of the new signal displaying two white lights and an 'X' in the theatre box.

Now, what to do for the best in the very unlikely scenario this really was a runaway?

The best platform to divert such a train to was platform one which stood some way back from the main concourse in the east corner of the station. The problem was, the platform was occupied by an evening commuter service, packed of course, due away in one minute. A quick decision was made to signal the train away from platform one to the down fast line. This choice was made because there simply would not have been enough time to evacuate the train and platforms, there being virtually no communication of the type we now enjoy between signallers and train drivers. There would also have been no chance to evacuate the station concourse. It was a huge relief when the train in platform one departed a few seconds after the road

ABOVE & BELOW:
Victoria Eastern: Victoria Eastern signal box was a 200 lever miniature frame, opened in January 1920. It originally controlled semaphore signals, but these were converted to colour light signals in 1939. The box closed in 1979 when control was transferred to Victoria Central in the short term, before the Victoria signalling centre, located at Clapham Junction, opened in May 1980. Perched to the east of platform one, this external view shows EMU No. 7147 in the platform that would have been used, had there been a runaway. The interior view shows the signal diagram and the 200-lever frame. Photos: Trevor Maxted.

came off, allowing a quick change of points to set the road for the possible runaway.

Believing this was nothing more sinister than a huge mistake by the driver I waited for the train to come to a stand on the first ground signal he approached adjacent to the carriage sidings. From observing the track circuits it was clear the train had stopped so the road was set into its booked platform and ground signals operated – remember there was no way to contact the driver except on a signal post phone (SPT) and there were none on the ground signals.

The train then ran normally in to its booked platform and the driver was asked, by station staff, to give the box a call. The driver was astonished as to what he'd done, firmly believing it was a new move due to the recent re-signalling and he'd obviously misread re-signalling notices. Needless to say, it never happened again.

WISBECH TO WHITEMOOR JUNCTION IN THE GUARD'S VAN

In the summer of 1981, I was rescued by a combination of a kindly driver and guard and the signalman at Whitemoor Junction. With college finished, a day out was planned to Ely, King's Lynn, South Lynn, Wisbech and March. The freight-only line between Wisbech and March was the main target of the day out and to get there it was necessary to load my bicycle on to the train from Cambridge to King's Lynn and then cycle along the A47 to Wisbech.

The plan involved trying to reach Wisbech in time to see the afternoon trip freight to Whitemoor which carried pet food from the Spillers factory and also traffic to and from the Metal Box company in Wisbech.

Everything was going to plan until a puncture three miles out of Wisbech. Unfortunately it wasn't any old puncture, but one which involved both the inner tube and the outer tyre splitting. After a 30 minute struggle by the roadside, I fitted a new inner tube, but had to limp along with a large bulge where the outer tyre had given way. Fearing another puncture, I half cycled and half pushed the bike into Wisbech, only to find Class 40 No. 40067 ready to depart with just the guard's van to attach to the 8J55 afternoon trip to Whitemoor.

I rushed into the goods yard to get at least one picture, only to be stopped by the guard who asked what I was doing. I explained that I had cycled from

King's Lynn to get a photograph of the train, but had suffered a puncture and was worried I was going to be too late to capture a picture of the train. He asked how I intended to get back to March, my next destination, with my bike in such a state? I said I hadn't thought that far ahead and he promptly went to speak to the driver and came back to suggest we load the bike into the guard's van and drop me off in March.

The details of how we would do this were worked out as we travelled down the branch line and I helped with some of the guard operated manual crossing gates.

Upon arrival at Whitemoor Junction, the freight normally pulled forward past the signal box, in order to reverse into the 'up' departure sidings.

On June 2, 1981, the driver paused opposite the box at Whitemoor to shout to the signalman that he was letting off a passenger with a bicycle so would draw forward, stopping with the guard's van level with the box steps. Not only that, but as his passenger had a rather heavy bicycle in the van, could the signalman pop down and help us unload it!

The passenger was offloaded, wheeled his bike to March station and caught the train to Cambridge, where the first stop was a bicycle repair shop on Mill Road.

ABOVE: The driver and guard of the 8J55, Wisbech to Whitemoor trip freight discuss how to get me from Wisbech to March back in June 1981. Class 40 No. 40067 has yet to attach a guard's van, needed for this air-braked freight because of several 'guard-operated' manual crossing gates along the Wisbech branch.

ABOVE: *Whitemoor Junction*: The view from the guard's van as we approach Whitemoor Junction signal box. With 147 levers this was the largest manual signal box in East Anglia at the time and had been double manned until 1981, until reduced traffic, because of the closure of the hump in Whitemoor up yard in October 1980, led to a change to single manning. Passengers and damaged bicycles were unloaded beyond the wooden fence to the left of the train, at the box steps.

LEFT: Staff at Whitemoor Junction signal box were always friendly, even though the box could be very busy at times. Here, in 1978, I found myself treated to a cup of tea and digestive biscuits one afternoon and thankfully took a couple of pictures inside the magnificent 147-lever structure. The picture evokes a bygone age with the pot-bellied stove on the left, my hard-bodied, brown camera bag (which weighed a ton) and then The Sun calendar on the right, something which would almost certainly lead to complaints in 2014!

LIFE IN A COUNTRY JUNCTION –
A SIGNALMAN'S RECOLLECTIONS
BY STEVEN ASHLING

Having spent my teenage years 'trespassing' in signal boxes, I finally had the opportunity to 'legalise' my interest when I became a signalman at Reedham Jn in 1995. A few months earlier I'd started signalling on North Norfolk Railway too. Signalling School was very local, by modern comparisons, as it was held in Norwich. Now it is a residential course at the excellent training centre at York. Our trainer was a tall grey-haired chap with glasses resembling the entertainer Syd Little.

The course lasted eight weeks with a middle week in the signal box. Once complete I had a few weeks training at Reedham Jn before passing out.

It was now July and summer Saturday trains were starting, a far cry from the previous decade when traffic levels were much higher with trains to destinations all over the country, but nonetheless plenty to make Saturdays interesting. The rest of week was just an hourly Up and Down Norwich Lowestoft service with half a dozen trains on the Berney to Yarmouth. Unlike other signal boxes, Sundays were busier as the Acle line was closed so all Yarmouth trains came our way.

On my first day I had a points failure. 44 points are about 250m from the box and suffer from the heat. You can get the points over but the lock won't go in. With the aid of a bar you can go down, complete the job and get trains running. Failing that a point clip will do the trick if the blades don't close up properly. The bar lived by the points but the clip was kept under the box and was a heavy carry on a hot day.

Reedham Jn was a lovely box to work. It had 60 levers of which 29 were still in use. I did attempt to clean them all one day. I was on a 12 hour shift during a drivers' strike. I had washed the car, cleaned the box, and tidied my locker, now what? I got the first 20 done and felt quite pleased then saw the remaining 40 and lost heart.

The one thing a mechanical box offers which no modern building can is the closeness to the environment around you. You become aware of the changing seasons and weather, especially temperature. The signal wires expand and contract as the temperature rises and falls through the day. Signals further away from the box have wire adjusters to regulate the slack in the wire should you pull a lever and the indicator does not display an 'Off' indication.

Being in a signal box during a thunder storm can be interesting. The frame is earthed but if a signal takes a lightning strike you get sparks jumping along the lever tops. I have, fortunately, only seen it the once, which was enough. Where telegraph poles were in place, the lighting would be picked up and the block bell may ring. Some of the nicest views from the box are after heavy rain where the signals are lit by the sun against a black sky. As the seasons roll around the snow will come. We had gas point heaters and you hear them hissing and popping away.

The railway somehow always looks neater with snow on the ground. Driving snow was the worst as it blew into the points and overwhelmed the heaters. Snowmen, as they were called, local P-way men would be stationed with you to maintain the points. This was welcome company and reassurance that help was close by. The cold affected the points and signals as much as the heat. The signals used mechanical point detection which has, and rightly so, small tolerances so occasionally a trip outside to pull a wire or bar a point was needed. This was part of the job really, I was lucky to be trained by a chap who had worked the box for 20 years and happy to pass on his experience.

Being in the country there was no shortage of nature. Rabbits played on the track, occasionally disturbed by the local fox. We even had a barn owl. One dark evening its white streak flew past the window and gave out a screech. I wasn't ready for that and it took a few moments for my heart rate to return to normal. Before my time, there was a signalman there who used to put seed in the points and then wait on the lever for a pheasant to pop its head in – perfect birds with no lead shot in. However, the P-way did not appreciate this as

FAR LEFT: *Reedham Junction*: In 1998, Steven Ashling enters the details of a Lowestoft to Norwich train into the log at Reedham Junction

LEFT: *Sheringham*: Still addicted to the manual box – Steven works Sheringham box in 2014 as a volunteer on the North Norfolk.

the seed and heads and grease needed cleaning out, but I am sure a brace soon smoothed things over!

Our signals were still paraffin lit. The lampman would come every Tuesday to trim the wicks and fill the lamps. There was a skill to setting them up correctly. Wick too high and the lamps soot up, too low and the lamps will not last the week. Strong winds occasionally blew the lamps out. 54 signal seemed to be the worst affected. I am no fan of heights but somehow I didn't mind climbing signals. Once relit we didn't need to caution trains, so it was worth a few minutes to do it.

Facing points have to be tested every four weeks and our roster was four weekly, so I used to see the S&T when I was on early turn, usually a Wednesday. We would pull the points back and forth until their gauges showed all was in order. Minor adjustments were made when necessary. The weekly track patrol would take place. One P-Way patrolman had a poor leg and used his spanner as a crutch. We were convinced if he stopped track walking his leg would probably lock up. No matter the weather he was out there covering mile upon mile.

Reedham Junction was a time capsule, with the exception of a modern sink unit it had not really changed in appearance in 50 years. We had a coal stove which made it very cosy in winter if not a little dusty. On a winter's evening I would be sat at the end of the frame looking out of the window into the dark, the red and

yellow dots of the signals marking a permanent constellation, there was little light pollution. People say oil lamps were not as good as colour lights, I do not dispute that but a well set-up lamp will reflect off the rails. The fire hissing, clock ticking and box dimly lit with just a light over the train register and the outside light over the stairs. This was heaven and I was paid to be there.

Sadly, after four very happy years it was time to move on. The Sheringham line was due to be re-signalled and we would probably be next. Having two trains an hour was starting to become a little boring and I needed something else. Reedham is due to close in 2016 so it lasted a further 17 years. My railway career has continued to be enjoyable, I have had the chance to make a difference and work with some great people over the last 20 years.

I have worked in an IECC and managed a powerbox, I am now working with Traffic Management System and ETCS development. While these fascinate me greatly, I love signalling, the mechanical signalbox has character and is where I am most content.

This is my story of my short time in signal box. Across the country you will find similar people who feel equally passionate about theirs, and rightly so. In a decade or so this way of life will be as lost as that of the lighthouse keeper, so it is important we preserve what we can and record the memories while we can.

ABOVE: *Attleborough*: David Hilton on the phone in Attleborough signal box with the fire going in the corner and the comfortable signalman's chair in evidence. The seats behind David were used to accommodate the frozen passengers in January 2012.

WARMTH AND SHELTER IN NORFOLK

Just as the loss of the station booking office has taken away the personal touch when booking tickets or asking for information, so the closure of hundreds of manual signal boxes has further de-personalised the public face of railways. The drive to reduce operating expenses and streamline signalling is one thing, but what about the human touch?

Back in winter 2011, I found myself waiting for the 0652 from Attleborough to Cambridge. The temperature on the 'up' platform at Attleborough was minus five degrees that January morning and the indicator board informed us the train was 25 minutes late. We stomped (myself and four other passengers) up and down the platform to keep our feet warm. Suddenly the reassuring voice of David Hilton (the signalman at Attleborough on that shift) came over the PA: "For passengers on platform 1, the train is 25 minutes late and I know it's freezing out there, if anybody wants to come and warm up in the signal box and have a cup of tea they are very welcome!"

All except one hardy soul, headed east to the signal box where, true to his word, David had a pot of tea ready for us. Not only that but we stayed in the box until after he had closed the gates for the approaching train because of the interlocked passenger gates which allowed passengers to cross the line at the signalman's discretion, even after the main gates were closed.

In 2014 we would simply freeze, the electronic display on the station has been more often out of order than not, since resignalling took place in 2012, and there are no longer passenger gates... so missing the train due to the barriers down is a common occurrence – they call it progress.

Another problem area, engendered by closure of crossing boxes, is obstacle detection.

In the old era, the signalman didn't close the gates if a mother was pushing her buggy across the road, or a group of children were dawdling home from school. One solution to the problem was the introduction of

CCTV, controlled from a distant box, but still observed in real time by the signalman. Various other solutions were investigated to make sure that nobody got stranded on the tracks once the gates came down and the simplest appeared to be radar, used in Germany, Switzerland and Austria. The radar systems were visited and a decision was made to employ this apparently safe and inexpensive technology on the Ely to Norwich line. This was resignalled by Signalling Solutions in 2011 and 2012 and was to be a showcase for how to modernise a line at much reduced cost by using 'plug and play' technology.

A problem arose in a senior project meeting at Network Rail when it was realised that the radar only swept from 18 inches above the ground. Then a member of the team asked what happens if a dog or a cat are on the tracks, or worse still a toddler? There was silence. Unlike in Germany or Switzerland, where if you trespass on the tracks, you are responsible, the legal position in the UK is that Network Rail may be found liable if it didn't protect you from the tracks by appropriate fences and safeguards – crazy, but true.

There was a crisis until somebody suggested a second set of low level radar (or Lidar), to make sure nothing could slip through the radar (which had been working without incident on the continent for years). These extra radar sensors were installed, but an unforeseen problem arose, first at Shippea Hill crossing near Ely and then all over Norfolk when it snowed in December 2012.

At Shippea Hill, which is on a curve, it was found that mud from the many sugar beet lorries, sprayed on to the Lidar, causing it to detect an obstruction on the crossing and therefore stop the gates being lowered. This caused chaos during the first few months of the Norwich to Ely resignalling as the only solution to get trains running was for the mobile operations manager to go out and clean the lens on the radar.

Worse was to come during the snows of December 2012 and January 2013.

Snow blocked all the Lidar machines, bringing the line to a standstill. So bad was the situation that the

ABOVE LEFT: *Attleborough*: Attleborough signal box, towards the end of its working life, October 2012. By this time, visits to the line by enthusiasts were a daily occurence and there was almost a party atmosphere with tea dispensed to many visitors. Here, my mother watched David in action one weekend as he invited us up into the box to show us how it worked as we waited at the station for a passing steam special. David spent his holidays operating signal boxes on the North Yorkshire Moors Railway – a veritable 'busman's holiday'.

Attleborough

contractors had to re-man all the crossings for several weeks and operate the barriers manually until a solution could be found. Eventually a retractable visor was devised, as seen in the picture of Attleborough crossing. This has a default position covering the Lidar lens, but once a crossing sequence is initiated by an approaching train, the cover retracts, the crossing is scanned and the barriers lowered. Once the train has passed and the barriers are raised, the cover comes back in place to protect the Lidar from mud, spray or snow.

Such trials and tribulations are to be anticipated with any new technology, but this seems to have been an unusually tortuous sequence of events. So much so, that in 2014 when the Dorset line was resignalled, there was a return to CCTV to control the crossing between Wareham and Poole.

AVOIDING DELAY THE OLD FASHIONED WAY – OR... 'PHONE A FRIEND'

About 15 years ago I had been invited to London to give an important lecture. Hurtling south-west at 90mph aboard the 0800 Norwich to Liverpool Street, I was enjoying a hearty Great Eastern breakfast. As we approached Stratford, the brakes came on and we ground to a halt.

The guard came through the restaurant car and informed passengers that there had been an incident at Maryland. I realised I wasn't going to make it to my lecture, so I phoned the only signalman I knew, who just happened to be at work on the early turn at Liverpool Street panel.

I explained my dilemma and he cheerfully told me: "Don't worry, there's a crossover on to the slow lines just in front of you, you're really lucky the two trains in front of you are past it, but I can slip you on to the slow lines now and you'll only be 10 minutes late".
No sooner had he said this than the train brakes were released and sure enough we crossed on to the slow lines. My fellow diner in the two seater table looked at me agog: "Did you really just make that happen he exclaimed!".

Yes it's not what you know but who you know that counts I joked. The other services caught behind what turned out to be a suicide were delayed over two hours.

I'm not sure the new Traffic Management System would allow the bold move that my signaller friend made, unless of course the computer algorithm showed he'd improved things for all the other services!

ABOVE: *Attleborough*: This view from summer 2014 shows the Grade II listed Attleborough signal box with the new automatic crossing gates. To the right of the view, the Lidar sensors can be seen with their lenses uncovered, as the crossing sequence has just been initiated by a Norwich to Cambridge train, which is two to three minutes away.

COOKING UP A STORM AT GREAT ROCKS JUNCTION

Great Rocks Junction signal box was built in 1923 by the Midland Railway and in the 1960s had its classic gabled roof replaced with a flat roof. It has 34 levers and had its windows modernised with UPC replacements in 2004. The levers are now classified as in table 1 (page 122).

The signal box has four 'residents' or permanent staff. I was fortunate to shadow Alex Fisher, a 10-year veteran who considers himself a relative 'new boy' on the railway for a couple of day shifts and one night shift.

Alex started work as a signalman after studying business management and entrepreneurship at university. Alex's first job on the railway was at Pinxton signal box but when this closed in August 2007, he moved to Lowdham box on the Nottingham to Newark line. Four years ago, Alex took the opportunity of a resident post at Great Rocks, a 45 minute drive from his home near Matlock. With Alex on the residents roster are Stuart Hicken, a 25-year veteran from Hindlow, and two newer recruits, John Burn, who transferred from

Sleaford when the Joint line was resignalled last year and John Pitchforth from Stockport – who has been at Great Rocks for two years.

Since March 2014, the shift pattern at Great Rocks is based on 12 hour days from 0600 to 1800 and 12 hour nights from 1800 to 0600. Prior to this, the box operated a more traditional three shift pattern of 0600-1400, 1400-2200 and 2200-0600. With the current roster a two week pattern unfolds with three days on, followed by four off, then four days at work and three days off. This roster keeps all four residents fully employed, so that annual leave and unexpected absences from work are covered by the High Peak Forest relief signallers, Nigel Ankers, David Styles, Gary Steer and Michael Orton. There are also two Furness Vale relief signallers, Malcolm Ashworth and Stuart Collier. All these relief signallers are passed out to work at Great Rocks Junction as well as Buxton, Chapel-en-le-Frith, Furness Vale, Norbury and Peak Forest South.

A relief signalman is somebody who has no permanent position in a particular signal box, but instead has learned several boxes in an area defined

BELOW: *Great Rocks*: Class 60 No. 66010 had passed Great Rocks 35 minutes earlier with the 6H06, Lostock Hall to Tunstead empty limestone train, and is seen here returning light engine to Peak Forest stabling point. Signalman Fisher stretches to collect the token for the single line.

by a specific mileage radius from the designated home signal box. A 'relief' is therefore able to cover for colleagues when they are away on holiday. The relief also covers for sick days, unexpected leave, assessment days and even paternity leave. Overseeing the whole area at the time of my visits was local operations manager (LOM) Anthony MacIntyre. He co-ordinated the staff from the signal boxes at Great Rocks, Peak Forest, Buxton, Chapel-en-le Frith, Furness Vale, New Mills South Junction and New Mills Central, not forgetting Norbury Hollow Manual Gated Crossing.

In one of those wonderful twists of fate, I had photographed the old gas lamps in Denton Junction signal box back in 1984, when the signalman was none other than Anthony. Back in those days it was my habit to print out an image of the signal box to post to the signalman – thus fast forward to 2012 and Anthony immediately recognised my name when I arranged a visit to Great Rocks. Sadly he had lost my old print but in these days of scanners and email it took just moments to dig out the old negative and scan it to email – how things have changed.

The shift begins for Alex with a 45 minute drive, through the Peak District from his home near Matlock. As a handover is always needed, Alex arrives on average 10 minutes before his shift officially starts, parks up and unloads provisions for the shift. When I first spent the day at Great Rocks, Alex had brought double portions of 'boil in the bag' cod in a creamy sauce for a luxury supper at the end of the day. Sadly, I had booked into a bed and breakfast in nearby Castleton, so was expected for supper there – I never did taste the cod! On my night visit a large bag of croissants was provided for an early breakfast with coffee. Handover on June 18 was with Stuart Hicken, who confirmed that 6M98, the Tunstead to Wellingborough stone train was standing at the exit signal from Tunstead, ready for an on time departure. Otherwise, all was quiet. In particular there were no 'possessions' or problems on the patch and no workmen that Alex needed to be aware of.

Within minutes of Stuart's departure, the kettle was on. Signalmen the world over thrive on lashings of tea or coffee, and in Alex's case strong tea was the order of the day. Alex also keeps certain traditions alive in that he eschews the electric kettle in favour of a more traditional one which sits on the stove and whistles when it boils.

Talking of strong tea or coffee to remain awake through the small hours, it is worth noting the strict regulations surrounding signalmen and women. They work in a safety critical job, unsupervised and often alone for 12 hours. There is a zero tolerance policy to alcohol and any other recreational drugs and the blood alcohol level of a signalman must be zero at all times when he/she is at work. There is also a rigorous monitoring system for medication which is managed by the LOM. Any signaller who has a new tablet or even takes over-the-counter medicine for a cold must report it

ABOVE: *Great Rocks:* Into the oven for the sausages and potatoes. Alex starts to cook his legendary Saturday morning fry-up.

to their LOM, who then uses Network Rail's pharmacist on-call system. Indeed, those with medical knowledge might find the system too draconian. I have known of a young man who hurt his knee playing football on Saturday and who bought some Solpadeine from the chemist for the pain. This contains paracetamol and just a small dose of codeine. Because the codeine has the potential to cause drowsiness and, rarely, hallucinations, the poor man was barred from work until he had seen a doctor at BUPA (Network Rail uses BUPA for all urgent appointments to try and provide the most efficient medical care for staff).

I have from time to time questioned the use of non-medical advice which does lead to more exclusions from work than might be necessary, however, I understand a cost benefit analysis by Network Rail suggests using the medical advisory services that are available would cost more than it might save.

Accountancy rules all our lives – who remembers the 'U-bahn' concept where it was decided back in 1989 that the cheapest way to get a wagon from Doncaster to Warrington was via the North London Line? Whatever the failings, there is no doubt that Network Rail takes safety extremely seriously.

Back to Great Rocks, where the most dangerous drug is Alex's tea!

In the last 18 months, I have been privileged to observe several day shifts and one night shift at Great Rocks. Not only that but I have visited the area many times over the last 40 years.

My son and I spent a sybaritic evening in Great Rocks signal box back in 1990 and it was from here in 1990 that I was persuaded to ride in the cab of a Class 47 to Northwich and back (much to the disgust of my family who were staying in a holiday cottage in Buxton). Great Rocks really is a special place.

Arriving for the night shift, Alex brings the necessary food as I have already mentioned. The 6M98, Tunstead to Wellingborough is standing at the signal in the departure road from the quarry, but isn't due out until 1830, otherwise all is quiet. Stuart leaves and as we have 45 minutes Alex boils the kettle and begins to prepare supper – his favourite boiled potatoes and fish. Having experienced the offer of boil in the bag cod before, I had eaten near Chatsworth on my way to the box, so didn't have to trouble Alex with cooking for two.

Supper was prepared on the Network Rail Baby Belling stove and smelled delicious. I contented myself with a cup of tea and one of the pastries that Alex had brought to provide fuel through the night. Alex's LOM, Anthony MacIntyre, once recounted to me that when he worked a box, a full English fry-up was the order of the day on Saturday mornings, sandwiches normally for the late turn shifts and white bread toasted and dripping with butter on nights... no margarine here, he exclaimed. The Saturday morning fry-up was something I was to witness on a later visit to Great Rocks.

In the background, the birds are singing. Radios, televisions, mobile phones and games consoles are all banned in signal boxes as they could cause unnecessary distraction in what is a safety critical job. The conversation is intense about what the railway used to be like when suddenly the phone rings. It's 6M98. It's 1828. The driver has been sitting in his GB Railfreight Class 66 for nearly two hours, but now wants the road, just two minutes prior to his booked time. Everything stops as the road is set, the train is belled on to Peak Forest Box and an on time departure at 120 seconds notice is organised. This is the life of a signalman. Both Alex and the driver know that 6M98 needs to be away at 1830 and is standing at the signal, but not until the driver confirmed he was ready to depart could things happen.

The evening is busy with further trains, a Tunstead to West Thurrock, a Peak Forest to Stourton which on this occasion had to run round via Great Rocks due to some of Peak's sidings being out of use, shunting movements from Peak Forest which impinge on Great Rocks, a Bredbury to Tunstead and then the classic Lostock to Tunstead empty lime (6H06). I'm not sure Alex even finished his supper. As 2300 approaches, the single line token machine in the corner of the box, which had previously stood sentinel in an awkward silence, sprung to life with a metallic 'dink'.

The Buxton signaller was calling Alex's attention with a single bell and offering a light engine which had originated from Dowlow and was bound for Peak Forest sidings. As Alex acknowledged the 2-3 bellcode from Buxton, he held the button in on the final ding in order to allow the Buxton signaller to remove a token from the machine at his end. After around 20 minutes, the lights of the locomotive slowly came into view around

ABOVE: *Great Rocks:* Alex Fisher perches on the frame at Great Rocks signal box in June 2014 as he takes 'handover' from Stuart Hicken, who has been resident at Great Rocks for 25 years.

BELOW LEFT: In April 2014, Class 60 No. 60010 has the throttle fully open as it climbs at 10mph past Great Rocks with 6F05, the evening limestone train from Tunstead to Oakleigh. To the right of the locomotive is the block token instrument for the single-line section to Buxton.

the curve and with the road set and the train accepted by Peak Forest, Alex was able to don his high visibility vest and saunter down the box steps to retrieve the token from the driver and upon his return the whistling kettle signifies the time for another – our fourth – cup of tea.

The locomotive has the single line token from Buxton which Alex collects as it passes the box. The token is then inserted into the red token machine at Great Rocks and the 'train out of section' bellcode is sent to Buxton. Until this is done, neither Alex, nor his colleague at Buxton can release another token from the block instrument to allow another loco or train on to the stretch of single track between Buxton and Tunstead. An area of confusion for many railway enthusiasts is the difference between a single line token and a One Train Working staff. With a 'staff' there is only one of them in existence and when the driver has the staff he has free reign on the single line. The driver must however return to the point where the staff was issued before it can be reissued to another train.

With a token, there are many in existence, lodged safely in two or more interlocked 'block token instrument'. While only one can be free at any one time, they can be returned to either of the machines at the ends of the single line, or one of potentially several intermediate token machines and thus another train can then enter the single line regardless of where the first train ended up, provided of course that it was completely clear of the single line. Thus as trains and locomotives regularly pass along the line between Great Rocks Junction and Buxton, the token system is in operation and until its closure there was even an intermediate token machine at Topley Pike which allowed trains to serve the quarry while others passed by on the single line.

For the line between Great Rocks Junction and Buxton, the token system is in operation, as compared with the old Corton Wood colliery branch near Wath (a favourite of Alex) where a staff was used.

Talk returns to "how it used to be" and Alex's obsession with Wath yard comes to the fore. Being more than 20 years younger than me, he has never seen

Table Two: 24 hours at Great Rocks – July 1, 2014		
From	To	Time at Great Rocks Junction
Tinsley Yard (Fhh)	Tunstead Sidings	0137
Tunstead Sidings	Pendleton (Brindle Heath)	0200
Tunstead Sidings	Hope (Earles Sidings) Fhh	0217
Drax power station	Tunstead Sidings	0604
Peak Forest South SS	Briggs Sidings Steetley Coy	0727
Pendleton (Brindle Heath)	Tunstead Sidings	0947
West Thurrock Sidings Fhh	Tunstead Sidings	1019
Tunstead Sidings	Briggs ICI Sidings	1149
Guide Bridge Yard (Flhh)	Tunstead Sidings	1243
Briggs Sidings Steetley Coy	Ashburys SS	1403
Tunstead	Bredbury Tilcon	1600
Briggs I.C.I. Sidings	Tunstead Sidings	1614
Tunstead Sidings	Hope (earles Sidings) Fhh	1745
Tunstead	Briggs ICI Sidings	1837
Willesden Euroterminal	Tunstead Sidings	1908
Briggs ICI Sidings	Tunstead Sidings	2256

Note – during this 24 hours there were 16 freight services handled by Great Rocks Junction signal box as compared to 24 at Peak Forest Sorting Sidings box, just under a mile north. This reflects eight extra aggregate services from the Dove Holes Quarry to the north of Peak Forest Sidings, which do not make it as far south as Great Rocks Junction.

Table One: The lever allocation at Great Rocks – summer 2014		
1 –	W –	Spare
2 –	W –	Spare
3 –	W –	Spare
4 –	B –	Point Down and Up Buxton to Up
5 –	B –	Point Up from Down and Up Buxton
6 –	R –	WB shunt signal Up to: BLI/Buxton/Tunstead
7 –	W –	Spare
8 –	BI –	FPL for No. 4 Points
9 –	B –	Point Up to Down and Up Goods
10 –	B –	Point Down and Up Goods trap point
11 –	R –	WB shunt signal Down and Up Goods to: BLI/Buxton/Tunstead
12 –	R –	Shunt signal Down and Up Buxton to: Down and Up Goods
13 –	R –	Main aspect – Down and Up Buxton to Up
14 –	R –	WB Starting/Section signal Up towards Peak Forest South
15 –	W –	Spare
16 –	W –	Spare
17 –	R –	Shunt signal, Down to: Tunstead
18 –	R –	WB Main line Down to Down and Up Buxton to Up
19 –	W –	Spare
20 –	R –	Stop shunt from Reception Road BLI
21 –	R –	Stop shunt to Reception Road or Siding BLI
22 –	R –	Reception Road to Down and Up Goods
23 –	R –	Reception Road to Up Main
24 –	BI –	Bolt lock on Siding Slip (Blue)
25 –	B –	Up Main from Reception Road (BLI)
26 –	R –	Slot from Tunstead (Red)
27 –	R –	Ex Tunstead to Down and Up Goods
28 –	R –	Ex Tunstead to Up
29 –	B –	Reception road to Up Main
30 –	BI –	FPL for 29 points
31 –	BI –	FPl for No9 and 32A points
32 –	B –	Crossover Down to Tunstead or BLI
33 –	BI –	FPL for 32B points
34 –	R –	Shunt signal Mainline into BLI Top end

W White - out of use – (7), **B** Black - points – (7), **R –** Red - signals – (11), **WB** White band — Signals, Locked by the block signals (4), **BI** - Blue - facing point locks – (5)

the yard in action, so talk turns to what I saw and what I managed to photograph (and I wish it were more). As the small hours approach, things become quiet and I have to confess I may have fallen asleep. By 0530, the shift is drawing to a close and Alex's relief is close at hand. All is quiet and Alex heads home just before 0600 for some deserved rest, in the knowledge that by 1800 he will be back at Great Rocks for another shift.

The Network Rail plan to close all manual signal boxes as soon as possible has predicted that Great Rocks should survive until 2025, making it potentially one of the last Victorian era manual signal boxes in the UK. That said, cab signalling and other developments might have an impact on current predictions for self contained systems like the Buxton/Peak Forest area. Whatever the case, Alex recognises his privileged position at Great Rocks when all around him hundreds of boxes are closing, and at the moment his haven of railway sanity has at least another decade to operate.

Now, back to the Saturday morning fry up. At the end of the shift, Alex suggested later in the summer I should return for one of his legendary fry-ups. With a period of relative quiet for three hours, a summer morning was chosen. Sausages, beans, bacon, black pudding and potatoes were all cooked to perfection and we even had a white table cloth! It was like going back in time as the images of the morning show – there are still pockets of traditional railway and the characters to make them special, but not for much longer.

'LIVING THE DREAM' –
A SIGNALMAN'S STORY

BY JOHN ILLINGWORTH

I first visited a signal box at the age of 10. The entry for Monday, May 10, in my little red Walkers diary of 1969 reads simply: "WENT IN MAGHULL Signal box." I and my pal Phil loitered on the platform of my home town on the main line between Liverpool Exchange and Preston watching trains go by. I'd seen the signalman opening and closing gates, heaving on levers and pinging bells and had become intrigued. To be invited up to the inner sanctum as a 10-year-old was clearly momentous as the journal entry was made with double underlined capitals!

From that day I was always interested in this particular aspect of the railway. The whole feel of the places intrigued me, they attack all your senses:

- the smell of well buffed lino, oil and grease
- the sight of brightly coloured levers, polished wooden block instruments, gleaming brass work
- the sounds of bells pinging, levers crashing and gates clattering
- Victoriana alive and well and still earning its keep.

From then, whenever the opportunity arose I'd try and worm my way into a box. I cycled all over visiting boxes. Locally Sefton Junction, Aintree Station Junction and Bootle Junction were three which as a teenager I regularly visited and if it was with the right man on duty I'd get to have a go, closely supervised of course!

A MIDLIFE CRISIS

Fast forward to 2008 and I've moved from Liverpool to Nottingham and acquired a degree at Trent Polytechnic, worked for a food company for 20 years, spent another five years as a self-employed small time property developer then all of a sudden the world has run out of money and it's time for a re-think.

A speculative letter to Network Rail saw me enter the tortuous recruitment process that dragged on for over 18 months before finally seeing me start work as Lowdham GPR (General Purpose Relief) signaller as recently as Easter 2009. Twelve weeks of very intensive training followed at 'Signal School' in Leeds with a great bunch of lads all working towards various signalling roles throughout the country.

Once passed out your days are spent learning your new box. It is still necessary, however, to convince your manager you know your stuff so a further grilling over two lengthy sessions in the office ensued. The final fence to overcome was the signalling Inspector. This is no formality and good men have failed at this last stage. Fortunately I cleared that jump as well and was released upon the travelling public, flying solo for the first time at the idyllic Fiskerton Junction in September 2009.

Having passed out Fiskerton Junction a period of training then followed to learn the five other signal boxes and three crossing keepers' jobs that made up my patch. After three years on the job I got the opportunity

ABOVE: *Wrawby Junction:* Perhaps the ultimate box to work as a signalling and freight enthusiast – Wrawby Junction. John fills in the signalling log with yet another freight bound for Immingham Docks. Photo: John Illingworth.

to add Netherfield Junction to the list of boxes I signed. A Grade 4 box, this was by far my favourite, much busier, regulating trains and keeping you thinking.

Netherfield was also another box I'd visited and had a dabble at in my youth. As a 19-year-old student I lived just around the corner from the box and, as I had in Liverpool, I got to know one of the resident signallers. Way back in 1978 the signallers at the time told me that Netherfield Junction box had no future; Trent PSB (Power Signal box) was to be extended to Newark and would link up with Doncaster PSB. It didn't happen and 34 years later and there I was pulling those same levers. Derby EMCC (East Midlands Control Centre) extended its tentacles to include Nottingham Station and beyond such that Netherfield & Rectory Junction boxes eventually closed on Sunday, July 28, 2013. After just 15 months of settled employment working the three crossing boxes and seven signal boxes the effects of Network Rail's Vision for the Future saw my two most interesting boxes wiped off the face of the railway map along with the busy Sneinton Crossing Shunt Frame and the once mighty Trent PSB.

THE ULTIMATE JOB

I applied for a Grade 5 secondment for the role of Barnetby East GPR. Covering 18 boxes as varied as Wrawby Junction, Barnetby East, Immingham Reception and Roxton Siding & Goxhill, it was a job made in signalling heaven, yet for me made no sense financially. Life, however, is not a dress rehearsal and if you'd asked me which boxes would you most like to work in the country Wrawby & Barnetby East would have to be up there. I went for it... and to my surprise I found I had got the job.

Roxton was passed out in short order then it was time for the big one, Wrawby Junction. It's generally busy and can get very busy very quickly – apparently the biggest busiest single manned box left still working absolute block with full train booking. It took some learning; there were a couple of days where I might have wondered if I was ever going to get to grips with the place. Would I be skulking back to Nottingham with my tail between my legs? That didn't happen and the place was passed out a week before Christmas 2013. A year on and 13 of the 18 boxes are in the bag, the five outstanding are all grade IIs but a shortage of cover since the start of the summer holiday season meant no training undertaken by myself for several months.

On passing out any new location your mood initially is always a little apprehensive but it's nice to be on your own, not trying to second guess what the signaller who is training you would do – it is then that you really learn the box. As you become more comfortable with each new role you become more relaxed and appreciate your surroundings and what a cracking job it is. Different boxes have a different feel, each with idiosyncrasies, each box manned by its own resident signallers looking after their charge with differing levels of enthusiasm. The different shifts and seasons all bring a different feel to your working day.

Mornings; often a nice quiet start, arrive before the streets are aired, watch the sunrise and the world awake, track walkers and men in orange appear wanting line blockages and other such nasties. Afternoons; for most boxes, busy upon your arrival, see the world wind down, the rat race head home, the sunset. Nights; different again, quiet at some boxes with the odd barn owl or fox replacing the rabbits and birdsong of the day turn.

Idyllic summer days with the windows and door open, the ping of the bells floating across the surrounding countryside, birds tweeting. Compare and

ABOVE: *Fiskerton Junction*: John keeps his diary up to date on a quiet evening in Fiskerton Junction. The moody 'selfie' has become one of John's trademarks during his new career as a signaller.
Photo: John Illingworth.

contrast with the dark winter nights, rain beating like shot on the windows of your cosy little box as a distant twinkling blue white light is observed steadily growing in size until a train emerges, rippled through water dimpled windows only to recede into the distance as a diminishing red tail-light. There can't be many better jobs for a man who loves his trains, especially freight, and has a keen interest in railway signalling.

I see heritage railways offering 'driver experience' days where people pay for the chance to drive a loco. For me an afternoon in a signal box would be more my bag and the joy of my job is not only do I regularly get to have a go in some of the best boxes in the country with an intense freight time table but instead of me paying for the honour, they pay me.

"I've reached the top and had to stop, that's what's bothering me" (The Jungle Book).

Could it get any better? The truthful answer is probably not, I'm guessing my signalling career has peaked. Now Christmas approaches and my current bevvy of boxes are again living on borrowed time. My secondment has been extended to Jan 1, 2016, that's good I suppose but the North East Lincs resignalling scheme dictates that, all things being equal, the bulk of my current boxes are due to be abolished Christmas Eve 2015. Control will pass to York ROC.

For all signallers it's an unsettling time. My secondment will end and I can in theory return to my previous role. But Lowdham, Fiskerton Junction and Staythorpe Crossing along with Bingham & Bottesford West Junction will, if all goes to plan, also have been abolished. For others who aren't able or prepared to move there's voluntary redundancy or possible, currently unspecific, redeployment? Uncertainty abounds. Where will I be in 15 months' time?

Will I be on the railway? I guess so as I'm prepared to relocate and keep taking short term vacancies, but it is now seemingly just a matter of time for the traditional signal box and the men and women that inhabit them. That men still sit in boxes equispaced along a stretch of railway line pinging bells and tugging on levers in the 21st century is really quite amazing.

The ROCs are the future Network Rail is pushing relentlessly towards. Absolute Block or Obsolete Block as it's often referred to is becoming just that.

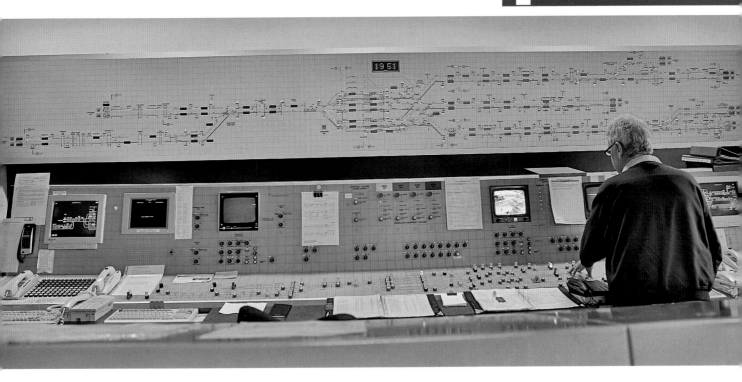

THE SIGNALMAN AS LATE 20TH CENTURY HERO –
A SIGNALMAN'S RECOLLECTIONS
BY 'ANON'

Derailment at Victoria Carriage Sidings and how to quickly recover the train service:
During an afternoon shift in the mid 1970s at Victoria Eastern I signalled a train of empty coaching stock, formed of 12 Cep/Bep/Cep plus MLV off an up boat train from either Dover or Folkestone, from platform 8 to the carriage sidings.

As the train was entering the sidings I noticed it had come to a stand right across the whole station throat. With that the phone rang and Cid the shunter said: "I think we're off the road." My immediate response was what do you mean 'think'?, Either we're off the road or we're not. Then Cid was a little more forthcoming and informed me the stock had been entering number one road, derailed and the leading cab was over by number nine road, quite some derailment.

It transpired a spring on one of the hand points had broken and the points moved as the leading bogie crossed it and the front coach at least was derailed. I asked the shunter if the unit of the leading coach which was derailed was clear of (inside) the sidings points and he confirmed it was. An instant decision was taken with the shunter to split off the partially derailed leading unit, get the driver to come to the station end cab and return the 8 car/MLV that was still on the track back in to platform 8. We were back running normally within 20 minutes of the initial derailment... try doing that today!

A BIT OF LIGHT RELIEF!
In the late Eighties and early Nineties I was relieving at Guildford panel box in Surrey. Back in those days, before the ridiculous privatisation of the rail network, most station announcers were situated in the signal boxes, Guildford being no exception.

A new computer screen system had been installed replacing the older 100% manual announcements with colourful display screens on platforms and in the station booking hall. Some of us signalman knew how to work the new equipment and one Sunday afternoon, when all was quiet, the late turn announcer had popped down the station for some reason.

Now it just so happened this was the day before a new timetable came in to force and Network South East, as it was then, was introducing a new allegedly super-fast service from Waterloo to Portsmouth with, I seem to recall, Guildford as the only intermediate stop. I think the train was 0730 from Waterloo and it wasgiven a flagship name, 'The Marie Rose', and this would be displayed on the station monitors.

With total devilment I said to my work colleague we can have some fun here and went in to the set up for the following morning and changed the name from 'The Marie Rose' to 'The Hairy Nose'. Of course, the following day at the pre-set time the train details popped up on the departure screens displaying the train title 0800 to Portsmouth Harbour, 'The Hairy Nose'! A few minutes later the station radios started to crackle and the supervisor was heard to say "get that nonsense off those screens". It was just a bit of harmless fun and we were told the passengers thought it was amusing, not something that would happen in today's corporate world!

LAST TRAIN TO 'THE NORTH'
As recently as 2014, our mystery hero has been helping the public and keeping the railway running. While on duty "in a signal box near you", he heard the station radio splutter into life as the station supervisor informed a platform employee in no uncertain terms that a poor lady bound for "the north" would have to purchase a new ticket as she had missed her pre-booked train. Our hero sprung into life and radioed the supervisor to ask – "did she miss her train because your 'up' Portsmouth was late?" "Yes"... "I see, so it wasn't her fault and you should help her get to her destination then should you not?"

All efforts were made for a trip via London for the poor passenger, including a taxi transfer across the capital. But for the intervention of an 'old school' signalman, the poor passenger would have been stranded south of the M25 with no recourse for the lateness of her connecting service – such is the fragmented and immature railway we now possess. ∎

ABOVE: *Guildford*: Trevor in action in Guildford NX panel, still working full time in his mid-60s and even filling in at Farncombe and other boxes, where he still has the knowledge.

Falsgrave*: Princess Elizabeth* reverses into the carriage sidings at Scarborough past the Grade II listed Falsgrave box. Built in 1908, the box contains a 120 lever frame. The splendid gantry here was moved to the North Yorkshire Moors Railway and stands at the north end of Grosmont station, all be it altered slightly. By 2010, when this view was taken, work was already well underway to move control of Scarborough station to an NX panel in Seamer West signal box.

Saving our signal boxes

In response to the Network Rail closure plans, English Heritage commissioned a report to look at which signal boxes were already listed. It then went on to consider which boxes should be listed to ensure as wide a spread of styles and makes of equipment were preserved for posterity.

The excellent 60 page report by John Minnis is available online http://services.english-heritage.org.uk/ResearchReportsPdfs/028-2012WEB.pdf

The author found that 94 signal boxes were already listed (see table 1 – page 128). Six of these while on the listed register had either been demolished or moved.

A list of a further 66 boxes where listing should be considered was drawn up (see table 3), but this does not guarantee a given structure will be successfully listed. One example is Spooner Row box in Norfolk. While it is a suggestion for listing, its fate has been very different.

The scholarly work by John Minnis concentrated on the design and manufacture of signal boxes, starting with the earliest Saxby and Farmer example at Billingshurst (see chapter 10), and trying to include examples of as many subsequent designs as possible.

In this chapter, however, I shall not repeat this process but have taken a different approach – 'The 100 Club'.

In table 2, I have listed all the signal boxes with more than 100 levers, many of which survive today and

LEFT: *Clapham A*: The 103 lever miniature lever frame across the northern approaches to Clapham Junction closed in 1990. Full details about this Westingouse miniature lever frame may be found on the excellent website dedicated to Westinghouse miniature frames: www.wbsframe.mste.co.uk/public/Clapham_Junction_A.html Here, in 1977, Class 47 No. 47203 accelerates up from Battersea Bridge with a Toton to Northfleet cement works MGR service. It is passing under the 1905-built signal box, into which a Westinghouse miniature frame was fitted in 1936.

Kings Dock Junction (Swansea): Controlling the entrance to the extensive sidings in Swansea Docks was Kings Dock Junction signal box. To the east was Swansea Burrows Sidings and to the west the coal drops and yards once so busy with coal exports to Ireland and the Americas. In this 1987 view, the 100 lever frame is seen as staff from the S&T department look at what needs doing to secure the 1908 Great Western structure for closure in a couple of weeks' time.

Shrewsbury Crewe Junction: Signaller Neil Hughes checks the tail light of a passing train leaning on the frame at Shrewsbury Crewe Junction signal box. Built in 1903 to an LNW design, it has 120 levers, and as just 40 are white or unused it has as many operational levers as the neighbouring Severn Bridge Junction.

Heaton Norris: The signalman is often a blur in the frantically busy Heaton Norris signal box. Built in 1955, the 125 lever box stands at the north of Stockport viaduct. This 2014 view shows in clear detail the 'centralisation' of the frame, such that just levers 31-90 are operational with banks of white levers at either extremity of the frame. This allows such a busy box to be single manned.

LEFT: *Londonderry Junction (Sunderland)*: Another large signal box controlling access to extensive dock sidings and coal staithes was in Sunderland Docks at Londonderry Junction. Built in the 19th century it had a 115 lever frame and fringed with Hendon Junction to the north and Ryhope Grange Junction to the south. Here, in August 1986, Class 56 No. 56130 passes the box with 6J70, the afternoon trip from Sunderland Docks to Murton colliery.

ABOVE AND BELOW: *Maidstone West*: The largest surviving manual signal box on the southern region is at Maidstone West. Hardly any of the 115 levers in the 1899-built box are needed anymore. In 2014, signallers David Peters and Reg Stevens are on duty.

Table 1

GRADE 2 LISTED SIGNAL BOXES – 2012

Ais Gill (Butterley), Askam, Attleborough, Baschurch, Beckingham, Bedale Beverley, Billingshurst, Birmingham New Street, Bollo Lane Junction, Brading, Brocklesby Junction Burton Agnes, Canterbury West, Carnforth Station Junc, Carnforth Station Junc (original), Chappell Wakes & Colne, Chathill Chesham, Crawley, Crediton, Cromer, Dawlish, Eastfield, East Holmes, Elsham, Embsay station, Falsgrave, Hale, Haltwhistle, Havant, Heckington, Heighington, Hertford East, Hexham, High Street (Lincoln), Holmwood, Horsham, Horstead Keynes South, Howden, Instow, Isfield Keighley Station Junction, Kilby Bridge (Butterley), Kirkham Abbey, Kirton Lime Sidings, Knaresborough, Leek Brook Junction Loughborough North, Louth North, March East Junction, New Bridge, Norham, Oakham Level Crossing, Oswestry South, Parbold, Princes Risborough North, Ruislip, Selside (Carnforth), Sleaford East, Shildon, Shrewsbury Crewe Junction, Shrewsbury Severn Bridge Junction, St Albans South, St Mary's Crossing, Stoke Cannon Stow Park, Sudbury, Swinderby, Topsham, Torquay, Wansford, Warmley, Weaverthorpe, Weston-super-Mare, West Street Junction, Williton, Woking, Wolferton, Worksop East, Wrawby Junction, Wroxham, Wylam, York station.

SWING BRIDGES

Boston swing bridge, Goole swing bridge, Sutton Bridge.

DEMOLISHED, WRONGLY CLASSIFIED OR MOVED

Burton Agnes (demolished), Ecclesfield (demolished), Feock (not a signal box – wrongly classified), Gorse Hill Bridges (demolished), Kettering (moved to Butterley), Nafferton (demolished).

included my selection of images to illustrate why these wonderful structures should be preserved.

The largest surviving mechanical box is at Shrewsbury Severn Bridge Junction. Since the closure of the 191 lever frame at Melbourne Spencer Street station, this is also the largest surviving manual signal box in the world and will certainly be preserved... but how many of the other '100 club' will we manage to keep as a reminder of Britain's Victorian railway?

Of course, as one industry insider put it: "We need a Dai Woodham of signal boxes." Certainly with enthusiasm and some lateral thinking, many boxes can be saved.

The recent Norwich to Ely line is an example. Wymondham box went to the Mid-Norfolk Railway, Spooner Row will be demolished but the top half of the

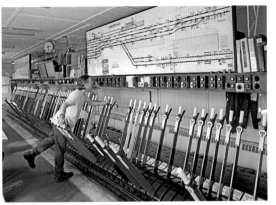

LEFT: *Stafford No. 4:* Signaller Thomas Larvin works the south end of Stafford No. 4 cabin for the busiest four hours on the late shift, having done the early turn at Stafford No. 5, which is single manned. No. 4 box was built in 1960 as part of the West Coast Main Line electrification, and has 105 levers.

Barnetby East: Not in the 100 club, but busy and fascinating none the less, Barnetby East hosted an official visit by the Railway Photography Circle in 2008. The signaller on duty looks on in amusement as his 72 lever Great Central box is photographed to within an inch of its life. Recording the vanishing heritage in such boxes will become an ever more pressing endeavour in the next five years.

Severn Bridge Junction (Shrewsbury): 'One hundred and eighty' – the frame at Severn Bridge Junction is the largest surviving manual frame in the world; this view from lever 180 gives an idea of its size. The box is listed (as is neighbouring Crewe Junction). Built in 1903 it is double manned because of the sheer length of the frame.

BRITAIN'S LARGEST SIGNAL BOXES (1986 TO 2015)
Table 2

SIGNAL BOX	DATE BUILT	DATE CLOSED	NUMBER OF LEVERS
Aber Junction	1953	1987	107
Clapham Junction A	1905	1990	103
Ditton Junction No.1	1956	Converted to NX panel 2000	100
Dover Marine	1914	1995	121
Falsgrave	1908	2010 (gantry moved to NYMR)	120
Fenchurch Street	1935	1995	140
Holyhead	1937	Open 2014	100
Kings Dock Junction	1908	1987	100
Londonderry Junction	Pre-1900	1986	115
Maidstone West	1899	Open 2014	115
Newton Abbot East	1926	1987	206
Newton Abbot West	1927	1987	153
Norwich Thorpe	1886	1986	125
Park Junction	1885	Open 2014	100
Pelham Street Junction	1883	2008	100
Radyr	1961	1998	107
Rhyl No. 2	1900	1990	126
Shrewsbury Crewe Junction	1903	Open 2014	120
Shrewsbury Severn Bridge Junction	1903	Open 2014	180
Speke Junction	1907	Open 2014	100
Stafford No. 4	1960	Open 2014	105
Stafford No. 5	1952	Open 2014	150
Stapleford and Sandiacre	1949	2009	115
Stockport No. 1	1884	Open 2014	113
Stockport No. 2	1890	Open 2014	120
Taunton East Junction	1931	1987	147
Taunton West Stn	1931	1986	135
Thorpe Bridge Junction	1899	1987	125
Totnes	1923	1987	111
Vauxhall SF (formerly Vauxhall and Duddeston)	1957	1992	100
Weymouth	1957	1987	116
Wimbledon A	1948	1990	112
Woking	1937	1997	131
Woodburn Junction	1929	Open 2014	104
Wrawby Junction	1916	Open 2014	137

RIGHT: *Stafford No. 5*: Built in 1952, Stafford No. 5 is much larger than No. 4 box to the south, with 150 levers. It is, however, single manned as many levers are white and not used and it does not have the complexity of a busy junction like No. 4. In 2014, signaller Thomas Larvin gets ready to end his early shift and has agreed to help out at No. 4 box for a few hours to cover for sickness.

Wrawby Junction: Built in 1916, and due to be decommissioned in 2016, Wrawby Junction has a 137 lever frame. The lever nearest the camera in this 2014 view is numbered 132, and there are five levers labelled A-E at the other end of the frame.

structure is to go to Cavick Lane Crossing on the Mid-Norfolk Railway.

Attleborough has been successfully listed and is cared for by the Attleborough Heritage Centre, adjacent to the station. Eccles Road box is to be demolished, but the lever frame is to be installed in the rebuilt Whitwell & Reepham box on the old M&GN route. Harling Road will again be demolished, but the lever frame is to go to the Wensleydale Railway. Thetford box was successfully listed at the suggestion of English Heritage.

Brandon box is to be demolished and the lever frame moved to Sheringham West box on the North Norfolk Railway. Lakenheath – the box in the worst condition along the line – is to be demolished, but even here the contractor says he may just store the frame in case anybody wants it. Finally, Shippea Hill has a stay of execution as it may be home to rare bats. Once the full detail of its importance as a nature reserve is clarified, it is hoped the frame will go to the Wensleydale Railway.

This remarkable achievement, saving all or part of eight from nine boxes, is the work of Steve Ashling, the former operations manager for West Anglia – maybe he should help other lines save as much of their signalling heritage as possible and get renamed 'Dai' into the bargain? ∎

Table 3
BOXES SUGGESTED FOR LISTING BY ENGLISH HERITAGE IN 2012

These are still all on Network Rail unless followed by HR when they are on heritage railways.

Arnside, Aylesford, Berwick, Bewdley North (HR), Bewdley South (HR), Birkdale
Bishops Lydeard (HR), Blankney, Blue Anchor (HR), Bodmin Road, Bootle, Bournemouth West Junction, Brundall, Canterbury East, Chichester, Cuxton, Daisyfield station, Downham Market Eastbourne, Garsdale, Goathland (HR), Grain Crossing, Haslemere, Haverthwaite (HR)
Hayes Knowl (HR), Hebden Bridge, Helsby Junction, Hensall, Highley (HR), Horrocksford Junction, Lakeside (HR), Levisham (HR), Littlehampton, Liverpool Street, Lostwithiel, Maidstone West Market Bosworth, Marsh Brook, Marston Moor, Monk's Siding, Norton South, Nunthorpe, Otterington, Par, Petersfield, Pulborough, Ramsbottom (HR), Ravenglass (HR) Runcorn, Rye, Settle, Shepherdswell, Skegness, Snodland, Spooner Row, St Bees, Thetford, Torre, Totnes, Tutbury Crossing, Uckfield (HR), Wainfleet, Wateringbury, Wellow, Woolston, Wye.

LEFT: *Stockport No. 2*: The larger of the two boxes that control Stockport station is the No. 2 box at the north end of the station. Built in 1890, it has a 120 lever frame; this has been reduced to just 90 levers, with Nos. 31-120 still above the frame. The smaller Stockport No. 1 signal box, south of the station, was built in 1884 with a 113 lever frame, now reduced to 98 levers. No. 2 box is seen in action here in March 2014.